THE EXCEPTIONAL LEADER

STAN TOLER

HARVEST HOUSE PUBLISHERS
EUGENE, OREGON

Cover design by Studio Gearbox, David Carlson

Cover photo © Comaniciu Dan / Shutterstock

Interior design by KUHN Design Group

For bulk, special sales, or ministry purchases, please call 1-800-547-8979.
Email: Customerservice@hhpbooks.com

This logo is a federally registered trademark of the Hawkins Children's LLC. Harvest House Publishers, Inc., is the exclusive licensee of this trademark.

The Exceptional Leader
Copyright © 2004, 2010, 2014, 2017 by Stan Toler
Published by Harvest House Publishers
Eugene, Oregon 97408
www.harvesthousepublishers.com

ISBN 978-0-7369-8074-6 (pbk.)
ISBN 978-0-7369-8075-3 (eBook)

Library of Congress Control Number: 2021949966

Printed in the United States of America

22 23 24 25 26 27 28 29 30 / VP / 10 9 8 7 6 5 4 3 2 1

"Stan Toler has written an engaging and informative book that will give the novice leader a mentor and the veteran leader a refresher course on how to balance leading with the head, the heart, and the soul. I highly recommend this book on becoming an effective leader."

JOHN MAXWELL

Acknowledgments

*Special thanks to Deloris Leonard,
Pat Diamond, and Gina Grate*

CONTENTS

FOREWORD

Leading is tough work, as anyone who has tried it for as long as I have knows. It's even more difficult to lead well. To become an exceptional leader is one of the greatest goals in life, so let your influence be one of excellence and lasting impact. Being involved in the professional sports business for many years now, I've had the opportunity to meet some very talented individuals. But big salaries, lofty roles, and glamorous publicity aren't what make a person great. Making an enduring mark with your life is more a matter of character and spirit than anything else. The big playmakers in life are the ones who help the rest of us aim toward a unified goal. That's what leadership is all about.

This is a must-read book for twenty-first-century leaders who want to lead with both soul and talent. Its narrative format makes it an easy read for busy people.

Leadership is more difficult and more in demand today than ever before. Yesterday's methods and mindsets are insufficient. I encourage you to savor the thoughts you're about to read. Don't just ingest them like fast food; let them marinate in your mind and soul. They have the capacity to help you be your best and to raise the level of your leadership to new heights.

—Jerry Colangelo,
Naismith Basketball Hall of Famer

INTRODUCTION

Whether you're in ministry, business, politics, education, or community service, people are talking not only about the need for more leaders, but also the need for better leaders. The rapid rate of change today has created a need for those who will lead at a higher dimension. Mere mental or physical manipulation doesn't cut it anymore; organizations and societies have evolved beyond traditional modes of influence. People want more. Effective leaders draw from five leadership realms, creating a synergy for change and organizational vitality. Throughout history many great leaders have led this way: with their heads, hearts, and souls. In today's world, this kind of leading is not optional if we are to be effective.

Many of us are intimidated by these gleaming, breathing leadership icons. Yet the principles by which they lead are within the grasp of most of us. For the roles that heaven calls us to fill, we have been given the ability to succeed.

This book tells the story of a contemporary sage who mentors a young leader who is in over his head. You are encouraged to eavesdrop on their beachside conversations and to capitalize on the journaling of Tim as he processes the main points of effective leading from his mentor, Paul. I've added some blank lined pages at the back of the book in case you want to make notes of your own.

—Stan Toler

1

THE LEADER'S MENTOR

Learning to Look for Logjams

Tim strolled down the long, empty beach, almost oblivious to the squawking seagulls, crashing waves, and misty morning breeze. His head swirled with concerns about work. Months ago, Tim had been selected as an up-and-coming leader within his organization. He'd been promoted beyond his years, which initially gave him an incredible sense of exhilaration. Now, things did not seem to be going so well. What began as a dream was becoming a bit of a nightmare. He didn't know what to do about the doldrums that had infiltrated his department. Notes he had written in his daily journal reminded him that things were not sailing along the way he had envisioned. The excitement of his people was fading, and no matter what changes and incentives he introduced, nothing seemed to make much difference. Although he would never admit it to his superiors or to those he led, Tim was beginning to doubt himself. Why had he been promoted to a place where he was unable to excel?

Every weekend for the last month, Tim had brought his wife and sons to the beach. His stress and long hours at work were taking a toll on his family, but at the beach everyone enjoyed the surroundings and playing in the surf. The bustle of downtown San Diego and the business centers of south Orange County, though just minutes away on the freeway, seemed far from this Carlsbad beach house. Tim's friend had given him a great off-season deal on the rent, and Tim welcomed the escape from the pressures of work and life. Even though it was temporary, it sure felt good for now.

While his wife and kids slept, Tim got up early, poured a mug of coffee, and walked surfside. Even Southern California beaches, packed in the summer, are practically empty during winter Saturday mornings. His walks lasted anywhere from 30 minutes to a couple of hours, depending on how much thinking got done. *Why is my organization*

stuck under my leadership? Why doesn't God give me the wis-
dom I need to be a better leader? Why do people always ask
why *when they are in a pickle? And why does God seem silent*
when you ask why *questions?*

Maybe heaven wasn't interested in the practical matters
of life—such as being an effective leader. Church, spirituality, and Scripture seemed far removed from the relevance of
work and business. *Maybe God doesn't really offer solutions*
for everyday problems—maybe inner peace and hope are all I
can expect, thought Tim. But lately, he had felt that peace
and hope were scarce. Perplexing thoughts had stolen the
joy he experienced at the beginning of a new challenge. His
emotions right now were like the tide: ebbing and flowing.

As he rounded the bend of the shore on his way back
to the house, he spotted an old man sitting on the deck of
a beachside cottage. He had seen the white-haired man a
few times, and they generally exchanged nods, waves, or
a brief hello. On previous days with the tide coming in,
it was difficult to hear each other over the crashing waves.
But today, Tim thought he should extend his friendship
a little further. As he came closer to the man's house, Tim
mustered a smile and waved. "Good morning!" he shouted.

"It sure is," the man responded. "Nothing beats an early
walk on the beach to clear your thoughts."

The man's disarming smile and penetrating eyes drew

Tim to the stairs leading up to the deck. "Yeah, it beats a therapist's couch. My family and I are renting a friend's house down the beach. We'll be driving up from the city for the next few weekends."

"Forgive me for being straightforward," the old man said, "but what do you think about when you stroll on the sand?"

"Oh, you know. Just work stuff."

"How are things going in your work?"

"Well, to be honest, things have been better. I received a promotion a few months ago, but lately I just haven't been cutting it." Tim surprised himself for going beyond the usual "I'm fine" response with the stranger.

"Ah, that's the challenge of leadership, isn't it?"

Tim climbed the stairs as if invited to come up to the deck. "How do you know I'm a leader?"

"Have a seat," the man said, motioning to one of the cushioned wooden deck chairs. "My name is Paul." He stood up slowly and extended his hand.

"Hi, I'm Tim," the younger man said as he shook hands and then sat down.

"I thought you might be a leader because I've worked with leaders for most of my life and, frankly, I'm pretty familiar with the look I see on your face," Paul said, his eyes twinkling.

"I'm not alone in my misery, huh?"

Paul laughed loudly. "Oh, every generation thinks it's the first to go through the problems leaders always experience: perplexing situations, self-doubt, dealing with people and with frustrations when things don't go as planned." Paul leaned forward in his chair. "Plus, the thrill of making a difference, of seeing your influence motivate people to accomplish what they could not do without your leadership."

Usually, Tim would have been irritated by Paul's assumption about his situation, but for some reason, he wasn't this time. The old man's nonthreatening style intrigued him.

"What did you do for a living, assuming you're retired?" Tim asked.

"I'm very much retired, but for most of my life I did one thing: I led." Paul leaned back in his chair. "First it was in the military, then politics, business, and eventually community and nonprofit groups. The last couple of decades, I've been a consultant to organizations wanting to develop their leadership. I've worked in large and small environments—both entrepreneurial and institutional settings. Leadership is pretty generic, though. The same principles apply to most groups."

"Wow, that's impressive. Maybe I could pick your brain a little."

"I'd love it. And you don't have to worry. Because I'm retired, I won't charge you the big bucks I used to get for my input," Paul said with a smile, leaning forward and tapping Tim on the knee.

Tim grinned. "So even though you don't know my specific situation, you believe I'm wrestling with something that's not all that unusual?"

"I'm not dismissing your concerns, Tim, and I don't claim to know your particular circumstances, but over the years I've observed that the problems of leading are common. Leadership is a natural process."

"Leadership is natural?" Tim asked. "What do you mean? It seems to me that leading is about going against the tide and bucking the trend. It requires a lot of effort."

Paul reached into a wicker basket beside his chair on the deck. He pulled out a seashell and tossed it out on the beach. "That shell fell all by itself, didn't it? I threw it, but the laws of nature—in this instance gravity—took over. Leadership often happens naturally. No matter where you go in history or civilization, you will see leadership happening. It's a natural social process in response to a personal need. Our creator instilled this need within people along with the capacity for cooperation to help them accomplish tasks together. We didn't invent leadership, and we don't have to force it. People want to be led well."

A LEADER DOESN'T HAVE TO CREATE LEADERSHIP. THE FORCES OF NATURE STRIVE TO LET LEADERSHIP HAPPEN.

Tim stroked his jaw as he tried to digest Paul's theory of leadership. "So if it's a law of nature, why are there so many books and seminars about leadership? And why am I having such a difficult time doing my job if it's natural?"

"I suppose it's the same reason you go to classes to prepare for natural childbirth," Paul said. "Natural does *not* mean effortless—or even easy. Birth, DNA replication, and photosynthesis are natural but incredibly complex processes. Diamonds are created naturally but only after years of intense geologic pressure. Waves are natural, but they can wreck ships, demolish homes, and tumble surfers like leaves in autumn winds."

"I'm still not sure I understand how leadership is natural."

"Let me put it another way. I have a friend, John, who was a lumberjack in Oregon. John frequently compares leadership with logging. In the old days, they cut down the trees and floated the logs on the river to the sawmill. The flow of the river did the work of hundreds of trucks. Sometimes, though, the logs would get stuck. Instead of going with the flow, they began piling up in long, compacted areas; you know—logjams. Experienced, skillful loggers could look at a jam and identify which logs were causing the problem. They walked out to those specific logs and moved them, which allowed the river to do its work to free the logs to float downstream. A primary job of a capable leader is to see where leadership is getting jammed and to free up the process. A leader doesn't have to create leadership. You're not doing something unnatural when you lead. The forces of nature strive to let leadership happen."

"Wow, that's a lot different from how I've thought about it. But if it's natural, why does it seem like there are so many problems that go along with leading?"

"Well, leading isn't easy; but then, neither is lumberjacking—even when things go smoothly. The perceived problem is that many organizations are undergoing stress and that the complexity of leading today is greater than in the past, but the basic tenets of leadership remain the same."

"Are the logs people, metaphorically?"

"No, the logs represent leadership issues, and the lumberjacks are the leaders. When leaders lead well, they get a lot of credit for doing very little, because leadership is a natural process. It's when leadership gets stuck that leaders are needed. They earn their accolades when they recognize the snags and do something about them."

"Hmm," Tim mused. "Thinking about leadership as a natural process is a whole different twist on things. I wonder where the logjams are among my workers and in their schedules and job assignments."

"Now you're getting it," Paul said. "I gather you're a quick learner. If we let leadership just happen instead of trying to make it or force it, our problems become far more strategic and less power oriented and manipulative. Allowing leadership to flow naturally opens your eyes to new ways of getting out of the way."

"When you consulted on leadership, did you focus on the way logs flow in the river, or did you look at the loggers?"

"Ah, good question," Paul said, smiling. "The key lies in training the loggers to understand the flow and to know where and how to find the hindrances."

Tim sat silently as he thought about Paul's ideas. "You seem pretty confident about these things."

"I hope I don't seem smug. I guess it's just that I've been a student of leadership for most of my life, and I've also observed the same logjams occurring over and over. The old 80/20 rule works here as well as anywhere. If you take care of the most common 20 percent of the problems, you'll remedy 80 percent of the snags. Leadership sinks when it runs into organizational icebergs. Like the *Titanic,* leadership accidents happen more by what you don't see than by what you do. What often gets blamed as the cause really isn't the problem when you look closely. Symptoms can be confused with causes. It's what we don't see that often gets at the problem."

"What are those 20 percent issues?"

Paul reached back down into the basket beside his chair

and pulled a starfish from his seashore collection. "A few years ago, you could find starfish all over this beach. Now, they've all but disappeared." Paul handed the starfish to Tim. "The typical starfish has five arms, giving the appearance of a five-point star. Leadership typically gets hung up in at least one or more of the same five areas."

"What areas are those?"

"Curious, aren't you? I like that. Tell you what, Tim, if you agree to meet me here for a couple hours the next few Saturday mornings, I'd be happy to share with you what I've learned over the years."

"I would really appreciate that, Paul. It's as if you've read my mind. I've been thinking a lot about my leadership at work. I feel as though I'm stuck. I'd love to get your advice if you have the time."

"As you know, time is life, Tim. It's all we have. What we do with our limited amount of time is what makes the difference. My time is at a premium lately, but I would love to spend a few hours talking with you when you come up here on the weekends."

"I'm grateful for the offer."

"All right, it's a deal. Meet me here, Saturday mornings at eight o'clock. No contracts, just a handshake."

Tim stood up and extended his hand to his stately new mentor.

"Excuse me for not standing. My legs aren't what they used to be." Paul took Tim's hand and shook it firmly.

"Paul, you're a godsend. I'll look forward to our meeting next week."

"You never know what you'll find along the beach. Have faith, my friend."

Waving goodbye, Tim continued his walk, stepping more lightly than before. Finally, he had discovered a leadership mentor.

2

THE LEADER'S MIND

Learning to Put On the Right Hat

The next week dragged for Tim. Several times he caught himself anticipating the upcoming meeting with his newfound mentor. Sharing struggles with team members or superiors was too precarious. He appreciated this unique opportunity. How lucky to have run into such a resource! On Friday evening, Tim's family made the commute to the beach house. Saturday morning, Tim was up at dawn and reversed his usual sequence. He took a brief walk first and then grabbed his coffee as he headed up the beach toward Paul's cottage.

Paul watched his approach with a smile as Tim walked up to the deck. "Good morning."

"It's a great morning," Tim responded, climbing the steps.

"I was hoping you would take me up on my offer. Sometimes we get cold feet or buyer's remorse after cramming one more commitment into our bulging lives."

"Not at all, Paul. I've been looking forward to talking with you." Tim sat down beside the white-haired man. "Things haven't changed much at work."

Paul shook his head slightly. "As leaders, we know that the best condition for change is, unfortunately, pain. Actually, you're probably in the best possible state of mind to gather some new insights."

"I kept the starfish you gave me last week. I set it on my desk at work, wondering what the five points of the star represented. It's an intriguing idea that leadership is a natural process, and my job is to identify the logjams and solve big problems with only a little effort."

"Bravo, Tim! You remembered the earlier meeting well. When I was teaching leadership at the university, I always wondered how much my students were taking home and how much went in the garbage as soon as they left the room."

"I'm all ears," Tim said, taking a small tablet and pen

from his pocket. "I thought I might take some notes if that's okay."

"That's fine," Paul said, adjusting his posture. "A five-star hotel or a movie that gets five stars is the ultimate. We want to pursue excellence in leading, so we'll pretend each appendage of the starfish represents one star of an exceptional leader. Today we'll talk about the first point of the star. A five-armed starfish makes this easy to visualize if you hold it vertically. The arm pointing up is a symbol of a leader's head, his mind. That's the first area we have to explore when a leadership logjam occurs."

Tim looked up, his eyebrows slightly raised. "What do you mean, 'a leader's mind'? I thought we were talking about organizations getting stuck. You know, where people plug up the process."

"I said we would talk about fixing the 20 percent of problems that create 80 percent of the challenges in leadership," Paul explained. "That means we have to focus on the leader, because it's the leader who is the primary catalyst for the social process we call leadership. Like the lumberjack, the leader must be the one to identify the logjams. Unlike the lumberjack, many of a leader's logjams occur within."

"But my team's problems are not in my head," Tim blurted out.

"People who want to catalyze leadership need to

understand the mind of a leader. They must understand basic organizational health and structure. When a leader fails to think like a leader, that person will stare at the collision of logs without a clue as to which ones are causing the jam. The mind of a leader is akin to the steering wheel of a car, helping to direct and to guide the organization."

"So when leadership fails, it's because the leader doesn't understand how organizations function," Tim summarized.

"Well, that's part of it. Certainly, the leadership process goes beyond the leader and is rarely as simplistic as a single issue. But of the five points of the star, we have to start with the obvious—how a leader thinks."

"How do you gain this knowledge and these thinking skills?"

"Experience is the best teacher. Other tools include books, seminars, DVDs, consultants, and mentoring, but knowledge only goes so far if you're not wired to lead."

"I take it you don't think everyone can become a superior leader."

"No, I don't. All of us can learn the basics of how leadership works, and we can lead effectively in certain contexts. We can discover disciplines necessary in leading, such as communication, strategic planning, and people skills, but aptitude is required to lead with excellence."

Tim looked up from his notes. "Then why do so many resources and speakers imply that anyone can lead?"

"It's the way we've been taught," Paul said with a laugh. He spread his arms wide. "This is a land of opportunity. It's unacceptable to tell people they can't become whatever they want to become in such a free nation. But we set up people to fail when we encourage them to think that way. The motivators who tell us that everyone can lead mean well, but they end up de-motivating listeners who fail in their attempts to lead and then wrestle with why they feel so inadequate. They think, *If everyone can lead, then why can't I?* Besides, the high pay and perks of leadership entice those who are ambitious to covet the title of leader. With so many people and books talking about the subject right now, we pressure people into trying to be what they aren't. Unfortunately, this causes those who are not leaders to think they're second-class people. Nothing could be further from the truth. You need exceptional followers as well as exceptional leaders."

"So…how do I know if I'm a leader?"

"My gut tells me you are, but based on the little I know about you, I can't be sure. One way to identify leaders is to look at their past roles, when there was very little structure, to see if peers looked to them for solutions and direction— such as in grade school, high school, church groups, and community involvement. You can usually see leadership aptitudes early in a person's life. Blossoming can happen later in life, but the leader's potential usually shows up in similar sorts of appointments in roles at work, in church, and in the community."

"You think leaders are born?" Tim asked.

"Well, of course leaders are born! Everyone is born," Paul said, chuckling at his own joke. "Probably the biggest myth in the business world is that *position* makes a person a leader. If a person gets elected or appointed and is given a new title, we assume some miraculous event takes place that endues the person with the ability to lead. That's a joke! Position no more makes you a leader than sitting in a forest makes you a tree. The tension comes when we expect leadership behavior from people in leadership roles but don't get them because these people don't think like leaders."

"How does one think like a leader?"

"Like I said, aptitude is the start. Researchers have proven that we all have gifts—specific areas of talent and strength our creator gave us in the womb. Our brain's neurological connections in the areas related to our inborn talents are like highways. Elsewhere we have the equivalent of cow paths. That's what makes some people great at sports, some at speaking, some at sales, some at construction, and others at leading.

"Aptitudes come in varying degrees. For instance, our word *talent* comes from a Bible story in which a talent was several pounds of gold. Three business managers each received different amounts of gold to invest. In this parable, one received one talent of gold, another got two talents, and the third received five talents. Each manager was evaluated on his own investment potential, not on anyone else's allotment. Many of our potentials—our talents—are God-given and blueprinted at birth. This represents capacity. Assuming that people have a capacity to lead, it must be developed and expanded. That's the benefit of reading the many fine books available on leadership, 360-degree analyses, mentoring, and education." Paul leaned back in his chair, allowing Tim to process the information he had just shared.

"Wait a minute. Are you saying a true leader has all the solutions already in mind to fix the organization?"

"No, I'm saying that a leader has the acumen to recognize when something is happening. Most people who are gifted as leaders *underestimate* the importance of the role leaders play within society. As a result, they take their own development far too haphazardly. They don't network sufficiently, read enough, or push themselves enough to stay on the cutting edge. Effective leaders are usually the first to recognize when there's a problem, whether it's a statistical decline, conflict in the ranks, or satisfaction with the status quo.

"Usually, leaders start immediately to investigate the cause of the problem. If they don't find it, they gather the team to look deeper or hire a consultant to turn over a few rocks. A leader doesn't have to know all the answers; none of us does. But he or she must be able to recognize when and where organizations get stuck and what must happen to identify the problem and develop a solution."

"Hmm," Tim said. "I was kind of expecting a recipe for fixing organizational malfunctions."

"If a cookbook like that existed, most of us would be millionaires. But bear in mind that leadership is an art, not a science. The best artists have natural inclinations, but they discipline themselves to learn their arts and develop their talent. The first and obvious area where organizations get stuck is in the leader's mind. When a person doesn't think like a leader, all sorts of problems occur. You can meddle here and there with peripheral logs, but others just keep stacking up. Ironically, the solution isn't in the water; it's in finding the logger who knows what he's doing."

"Wow, that current took me in a different direction than I thought," Tim said, smiling at his pun. "What should I do to think more like a leader in order to see the logjams in my organization?"

"First, become best friends with the business management section in your local bookstore. Learn to discern the difference between books on managing and those on leading. The latter is what you'll want to read most. Enroll in a leadership class or attend a seminar or workshop. Best of all, buddy up to someone who is respected as a leader from whom you can glean thoughts and who will serve as a backboard to bounce off ideas."

"With all due respect, Paul, it seems easy to say, 'think like a leader,'" Tim said.

"There are no easy answers. If you want to run a four-minute mile, you won't achieve it in six easy steps. You're going to have to run, pump iron, and push yourself through the pain. No one person can download all you need to know about developing a leader's mind. But I can tell you this: Not thinking like a leader is one of the five most common areas that cause organizations to get jammed. My job is to point you in the right direction. You have to do the work yourself."

"It seems to me that if you think like a leader, that would be all you need to succeed."

"Ah, that's where conventional wisdom stops, Tim. But, good or bad, right or wrong, that's only the starting point. Even talented, savvy, mentally sharp leaders err in other areas, which have to do with the other points of the star we'll discuss over the next few Saturdays."

Like old friends, they talked for nearly three hours. Afterward, Tim trudged up the beach to his house. His mind buzzed with more questions than when he had arrived at Paul's earlier that morning. But at the same time, he felt he was making real mental progress toward becoming the leader he desperately wanted to be. During the week, he expanded his notes into a new section in his journal, "Shells from the Mentor's Basket."

SHELLS FROM THE MENTOR'S BASKET

Shell 1: Be a Backseat Leader

What do you do if you discover that you don't have a natural inclination to lead, but you're in a role where you are expected to lead? Or what if you have an inclination to lead, but those around you are higher-octane types? Or what if you are a natural leader and desire to influence a situation, but you do not have the time or resources to lead?

The solution is backseat leading. We've all been influenced by people in our cars who provide input while we drive. We call them backseat drivers. We hold the steering wheel, but their comments, gasps, or information changes our direction and speed.

Business investors tell us how to make a profit using other people's money (OPM). Backseat leaders understand how to get things done by using other people's influence (OPI).

The following four questions must be answered by all leaders, regardless of the type of organization they lead:

1. *Who are the influencers?* These people may have formal or informal roles. A formal role usually involves a position, title, or organizational clout. Informal influence pertains to natural leadership aptitudes outside of official roles.

2. *What are the power resources?* People gain influence through a variety of means. These often vary in source and intensity from situation to situation and person to person. Recognize who has what influence within an organization: position (formal role/authority), charisma (charm/personality), expertise (achievements/experience), network (whom you know), information (what you know), or resources (wealth/strength/weapons).

3. *Who are the gatekeepers?* These are the people who are not necessarily leaders in and of themselves, but they have the ability to influence the influencers. They may be assistants, friends, family members, or respected peers of the influencers. Sometimes you can access gatekeepers more easily than leaders. No one makes decisions in a vacuum. We are all influenced by others around us even if we're not led by them.

4. *What are you trying to accomplish?* If you are not both clear and confident about what you want to see happen in the organization, you will probably have a difficult time communicating effectively. Passion and clarity are key elements to effective vision casting. Having an idea about how the leader feels and thinks about this same idea will greatly encourage the process.

Once you have identified these four factors, you can begin the backseat leading process. Always make connections with the influencers—directly, if possible. If you cannot access them, or if it would be detrimental to the outcome (because they do not trust, respect, or like you), then develop a relationship with a gatekeeper. When you have established a relationship, tell your story, opinion, concern, improvement, idea, or burden. Let the influencer or gatekeeper know how much you need his or her help.

History is full of scenarios where the people pulling the power switches were guided from the backseat. Don't underestimate the backseat's potential.

Shell 2: Become a Learner

Assuming you are wired to lead, your duty is to diligently hone your skills, whether your capacity is small, medium, or large. Leadership gets logjammed when leaders are not challenged. The best leaders in any field practice, rehearse, read, learn, assess, consult, and converse with other leaders. The human mind is an incredibly creative mechanism. The brain tends to pursue what is placed before it—good or bad. Our subconscious never sleeps. When we provide healthy brain food for our minds, our thoughts are activated to help us realize our potential.

Here is a quick assessment for an effective leader workout regimen:

1. *What resources on leadership are you availing yourself of today?* Inquire of respected leaders what they are reading, go online to examine leadership styles, read blogs of successful leaders and examine their skills and philosophies, and get into online groups that take leadership development seriously to develop your own leadership skills. Don't get stuck in the land of what used to be. Keep abreast of changes in culture and trends that affect your organization. What worked yesterday may not work tomorrow. If you don't keep up, your organization may be left behind.

2. *When did you last attend a conference to refine your leadership abilities?* Keep the saw sharpened. As you can, immersion in a live workshop or seminar on the same topic as a book or DVD will help you glean different ideas. A focused seminar will help you greatly. Plus, it will give you a break from mundane work issues. Being around people

who are learning the same things also provides invaluable interaction through give-and-take dialogue.

3. *When was the last time you did a measurable assessment on your team?* If the answer is more than one year, you are overdue and possibly in denial. A plethora of instruments are available for purchase. Annual evaluation in this area is invaluable.

4. *What type of mentoring program do you have in place?* Leaders who talk shop with one another improve thinking and discover new ideas. Mentoring primarily has to do with relating to someone who has more experience, who gives us more than we give them. Never underestimate the potential of hanging out with people who are going through similar situations. Pretending to be able to do it on our own is naive and shortsighted. It's dangerous to put off finding a mentor. (Remember, mentors become fewer as we grow older.)

Shell 3: Develop an Awesome Team

The growth process is hindered when leaders fail to develop their teams. In general, leaders who choose to work solo versus utilizing the abilities of the team set themselves up for failure. It's a proven fact that people working together consistently outperform even highly skilled individuals.

A great leader once asked a roomful of leaders, "How

many of you have deadwood on your staff?" Many hands went up among just as many chuckles. The noted leader asked, "Were they that way when you hired them, or did you make them that way?" Too many leaders blame the members of their team for not achieving personal excellence. Exceptional leaders assemble and *develop* effective teams.

1. *Pick good players.* Always staff beyond your strengths. Surrounding yourself with people who are your clones only makes your weaknesses more profound. Find people who can accomplish what needs to be done in your organization. Treat them well in terms of pay, affirmation, resources, and freedom. Do not be intimidated by hiring people who are smarter than you are. The excellence of the people you recruit and develop will reflect on your leadership.

2. *Direct traffic flow.* The difference between the present status and the future objective will significantly impact time, direction, and strategy. You cannot effectively know where you want to go until you know where you are now. A leader must point the team in the right direction. When you order an airline ticket online, you have to provide the place of departure as well as the city of destination. Knowing both of these allows the team to focus on the *how* and *where* of the organizational flow. Most people need to be pointed in the right direction.

3. *Recruit leaders.* If you want the organization to grow, stay on the lookout for qualified leaders and enlist them for the team. How do you pick those with influencing gifts and leadership aptitudes? Interview the person. Discover if there were childhood experiences of being the team captain, student-body president, or head bagger at the grocery store. Most leaders emerge early and provide indicators that they have potential. Observe how others look at the person. Do they seek out the person for input and opinions? Do they talk about the person when he or she is not present, noticing his or her absence in a positive way? Does the individual have a recent history of effective leading?

Shell 4: Do Not Just Manage—Lead!

Leading, managing, and administering are all supervisory roles that require making decisions that influence the effectiveness of an organization. Generally, people in supervisory roles get stuck in the managing rut when they should be leading. A flower in a cornfield is a weed because it's not what you are trying to grow. Leadership is not good management, and management is not good leadership. These are distinct yet necessary organizational processes. Bananas and apples are different from each other, but both are valuable members of the fruit family. If we are managing when we should be leading, we are lessening the effectiveness

MANAGING SEEKS TO PERPETUATE THE ORGANIZATION WHILE PROMOTING STABILITY. LEADING SEEKS TO EXPAND AND DEVELOP AN ORGANIZATION.

of the organization. These are, however, not black-and-white roles, and they often overlap from minute to minute, depending on the situation. That is why leading is such an art. Effective leaders discern when leading is called for and respond appropriately.

We need to discriminate between leadership situations and non-leadership situations. The most commonly confused supervision tasks are leading and managing.

Managing seeks to perpetuate the organization while promoting stability. Leading seeks to expand and develop an organization. Managing has to do with the maintenance of internal systems and programs within an organization. Leading is about changing an organization to respond better to the external influences on the work environment.

Managing incorporates goals, specific policies, and detailed plans for achievement. Leading focuses on mission, vision, and values.

Managing is primarily left-brain oriented. Leading strikes a balance between the left- and right-brain hemispheres.

Managing focuses on the *how*. Leading focuses on the *what* and *why*.

Many people assume they can learn to lead by shadowing a leader and watching what a leader does during the course of a day, week, month, or year. Unfortunately, that is insufficient because much of what a leader does is not leading. People who lead also manage, teach, promote, and market non-leader tasks.

Here are some questions that reflect leadership characteristics and can help reveal situations that require leading:

1. Does the matter at hand involve other leaders and influencers within the organization?

2. Does the situation require vision to be communicated?

3. Will policies and procedures be established that will significantly impact the future of the organization?

4. Will today's decision significantly influence the organizational culture?

5. Is it time for significant change in the organization?

Excellent leading involves making sure that effective management is in place, but it differs in nature and process from the role of management. If both leading and managing are being executed effectively, there is a healthy but dynamic tension between the two. They are oriented differently, but each is needed if the organization is to thrive. Too much of one without the other is not good over the long haul.

Shell 5: Wear the Right Hat

Exceptional leaders can evaluate and respond to a variety of situations that require very different leadership styles. Most leaders are limited to one or two styles of leading. Their dilemma is that an organization or team will eventually outgrow their limited response abilities.

Organizations vacillate in the type of leading they require, just as individuals need varying styles of leading within the organization. All leading is not the same. For example, if you respond too passively to situations that demand heavy-handed attention, people will lose respect for you and dismiss your influence. Follower insecurity disallows cohesive leadership. A leader who cannot respond effectively in a crisis will lose the faith of followers. Conversely, if you try to assume too much control in situations where mere facilitation is required, it will be like crushing a rose in your clenched fist. You will lose your best talent because colleagues will either flee or turn dormant out of fear of confrontation.

Here are four leadership hats, each effective in certain types of situations:

1. *General/Foreman:* This is a required hat when people are floundering. In these situations, time is of the essence,

and team members need direct, specific instruction as to what is expected of them. Times of crisis or acute lack of motivation require us to provide an easily identifiable *presence* within our organization. While you do not have to be mean to provide assertive leading, you do need to convey an attitude of urgency along with ample communication. If you appear overly relational or laid-back, people will not rise to the occasion.

2. *Coach:* When people are somewhat motivated, but lack information or direction, your role is that of a coach. You do not need to be as confrontational or assertive as a general/foreman because people on the team desire to be involved. Pushing the team may be necessary from an inspirational standpoint, but knowing strategies, implementing plans, and arranging players according to their strengths and abilities will raise the perceived competence of you as the leader and, subsequently, the players' respect for you.

3. *Team Captain:* Unlike a coach, team captains lead from within the game and are respected as peer leaders more than they are as top-down influencers. When people are generally competent, experienced, informed, and motivated, a leader must respond differently in order to be effective. A less assertive approach doesn't mean the leader is out of touch with what is happening. This type of leader is more proactive in development, planning, and

training. Encouraging team spirit and group accomplishment becomes the dominant theme of meetings.

4. *Friendly Expert:* If team members are highly competent and motivated, the leader's job is primarily one of facilitation. Some refer to these groups as leaderless groups, but that is a misnomer. Sometimes, an outsider would not be able to identify who the leader is because in meetings and interactions, this leader is more passive and more of a listener and observer. This does not mean that the friendly expert doesn't speak up and interact if needed, but the role is more like a consultant or informed peer than an authoritarian leader. Being too strong or opinionated at this level will crush leadership and render the leader obsolete.

Effective leaders will at times feel schizophrenic if they need to change leadership styles several times within the course of any given day, depending on the meeting, the conditions of the situation, and with whom they are interacting. Obviously, if you are limited to one or two styles of leading, you will reduce your ability to lead effectively in situations that lie outside of these appropriate styles, and leadership will be restricted. In effect, an inappropriate leadership style is the equivalent to pinching a water hose so that the water cannot flow freely from the nozzle.

3

THE LEADER'S MOTIVATION

*Learning to Ignite Imagination
and Communicate Passion*

How was your week at work?" Paul asked, greeting Tim on the deck.

"Well, it was intriguing, based on our last conversation," Tim replied. "I've tried to identify the influencers I know, what distinguishes leading from managing in my organization, and which hat to wear in different circumstances. I'm pretty jazzed about improving my understanding, and I've already purchased an interesting book and have found some excellent resources online."

"That's terrific, Tim! Nothing is as gratifying to a mentor or teacher as seeing a student taking action on new information."

"I'm a bit curious, though, to know what the other points of the star are. It seems to me, if you think like a leader and understand how organizations and teams operate, you're pretty much home."

Paul smiled and looked up at the wall of the cottage. "I put a visual aid on the wall for us," he said, pointing to a large starfish hanging on the wall. "I thought that since we're using our friend as a symbol, we might want to keep him handy."

"I still have mine sitting on my desk at work," Tim said, smiling.

Paul smiled back before saying, "When leadership gets snagged, certainly the first place to look is at the organizational understanding and talent development of the leader. But that's just one point. If you want to be an exceptional leader, you need to know the other areas that are vital to effective leading."

Tim picked up his tablet. "Shoot."

"The second point of the star has to do with a leader's heart—the source of the emotion, passion, and motivation that drives a leader. If the head is equivalent to the steering wheel of a car, the heart is like the engine."

"Why is the heart so important to leading?"

"Primarily, it's because leadership is a social art, and leaders are about influencing people. By nature, people are motivated by the heart, making emotional decisions far more often than logical and cerebral ones."

"How do you spell cerebral?" Tim said, smiling at his tablet.

"I just say it; I don't spell it," Paul responded with a smile of his own. "For example, what's the difference between a vision and a goal?"

"Well, I suppose a goal has to do with setting a hopeful objective, something you want to achieve. A vision is more of an overarching idea of what you want to accomplish."

"That's a great answer. I wouldn't disagree. But the biggest difference between a vision and a goal is one word: passion. A goal is like a dehydrated vision. It tells you intellectually what you want to accomplish, but it does not exude emotion or drive. Therefore, it's not contagious."

"Could two people try to accomplish the same thing, but one person pursues it as a goal and another as a vision?"

"Sure. Traditional definitions distinguish a vision from a goal in terms of specificity, exactness, and planning. A vision involves the big picture, while a goal is more defined. When JFK announced to America that he wanted NASA to put a man on the moon, that was a vision. The president said it in such a way that it ignited the hearts and imaginations of the American public. This in turn resulted in goal setting, budgeting, focused planning, and ultimately a man on the moon. And when Martin Luther King Jr. gave his 'I Have a Dream' speech, he communicated passion and electrified listeners. A professor teaching a class about the need to have ethnic equality might have said the same thing, but one spoke vision, the other a goal or principle. When Billy Graham stood up to talk to people about their need for God, his message was simple, but the intensity with which he said it made listeners want to come forward and make a commitment at the end of the service."

"I think I see the difference. But aren't you talking about communication and public-speaking skills more than leadership?"

"Nearly all effective leaders have effective communication skills," Paul said. "It's a fact that a leader can be persuasive without being visionary, but a leader cannot be visionary without being persuasive. Both passion and content are vital for effective leading. Vision poorly communicated is flat. People respond to passionate leadership."

"I've heard a lot of people in roles of authority talk about vision casting, but when they spoke, everyone pretty much yawned. What makes the difference?"

"Heart. The leader has to believe what he or she is

proposing. There is very little to gain when people propose something they don't really believe. Once, a renowned atheist was seen walking to hear the popular preacher John Wesley. His friend said, 'I thought you didn't believe in God.' The atheist responded, 'I don't. But John Wesley sure does.' Tim, I can't tell you enough how important the elements of passion and enthusiasm play within effective leadership."

"I suppose that's why when a leader loses heart, everyone is demotivated."

"I take it you've seen that firsthand. The leader is in charge of the thermostat. The leader sets the temperature of the room, and that is primarily a heart issue."

"But how do you *do* heart stuff? We're talking about an intangible. You can't just do passion or create emotion."

"It begins by being conscious of the importance of passion and heart. But it also means you legitimately have a vision and feel compelled to promote it. Most people don't have strong visions themselves. They rely heavily on others to help them develop a vision plan. When a leader fails to provide the motivation for the task at hand, then other priorities will take the place and consume the energies of would-be followers."

"But what about people who are passionate about things they don't know how to achieve?" Tim asked.

"That's where the mind and heart come together. If

you're all style and no substance, you'll raise emotions but not commitment. It goes back to having a leader's mind. The *how* follows the *what, why,* and *when.* The human mind is incredibly creative. We tend to discover the solutions after we have determined the destination and have bought into the possibilities. Leaders are not intimidated by the *hows.* They don't have to have all the solutions beforehand. Passion will ignite creativity within people, but you had better have some sort of plan to pursue the dream. Otherwise, people will eventually dismiss you as a hot-air salesman."

Tim leaned back in his chair and thought for a moment. Then he asked, "I hear what you're saying about passion, but is there a single way to engage all people?"

"Yes. The single way to light the fire in everyone is to ignite their individual passions." The old man smiled.

Tim knew he had been had. "Oh, great. How do you discover each potential leader's unique interest?"

"That's the task of the leader. You can gather the majority around a single, overarching team vision, but the glue that holds it all together involves helping individuals find fulfillment within the organization."

"That seems like a *mind* matter, not a *heart* matter," Tim suggested. "Finding people's talents and aligning them to the right roles."

"We're talking about more than strengths and talents. We're talking about the heart and motivations of people. This often coincides with, but usually transcends, talents and abilities. When people see how their personal goals and dreams can be accomplished through the corporate dream and vision, they will commit."

"What does that have to do with a leader's motivation?"

"Simple. Far too many leaders hamstring themselves because they are self-centered. At the heart of the problem is their motivation. Often, they think more about achieving their own goals instead of considering the hopes, dreams, and motivations of those they serve."

"Ouch. I thought leadership problems simply stemmed from organizational and environmental issues."

"A leader's heart has to do with his or her personal drive and motivation. There is nothing wrong with enjoying success and fulfillment as by-products, but when a leader is motivated primarily by selfish goals, others will not be motivated to follow. They will intentionally or unintentionally sabotage the outcome when they believe the leader does not have the team's best interest at heart."

Tim sat silently staring out at the ocean waves. Paul seemed content to let him think for a while. Finally, Tim took a breath and responded, "I hear you saying that leaders can experience logjam related to both of these issues—passionately communicating vision and seeing beyond personal motivations and drives."

"That's a good summary."

"Why don't we hear much about heart stuff?"

"I'm not sure," Paul admitted. "One reason may be because it's so intangible. We like to write and talk about leadership in terms of tangibles, to-do lists, and logical issues. Real people, however, are basically emotional creations, making small and big decisions based on feelings. I think another reason we hear little about heart stuff is because it's intimidating. It forces leaders to face things within themselves that they may not want to confront, and it's uncomfortable."

"I understand what you're saying, Paul. I've relied too much on my logical, intellectual approach to leading. I have grossly underestimated the importance of heart and passion in how I lead others. Yet I myself enjoy being in groups where the leader is motivated and personally committed to serving people and accomplishing the task."

"Serving people. That's what it's about, isn't it?" Paul replied, watching Tim closely.

"I think so. People want to know that the leader is committed to their best interests and is available to help them reach their personal goals on the way to achieving group objectives. When I sense that a leader is self-serving and just using me for his ego, I get turned off."

"So turn up the thermostat. Focus more on the hearts of people than their heads."

The hours passed before they knew it, and the session ended quickly. With his heart swirling with positive hope, a highly motivated Tim marched down the beach to mull over his thoughts.

SHELLS FROM THE MENTOR'S BASKET

Shell 1: Provide Clear, Sensory Vision to Ignite the Soul

People think in terms of pictures, not words. Merely stating a goal is not enough to garner the support and emotional stamina necessary to endure the challenges of any significant task. Storytellers have long understood the power of a well-told tale to ignite their listeners' emotions. Great communicators throughout history have implemented the practice of including anecdotes in their speeches. Jesus commonly used parables, metaphors, and allegories to communicate principles. The leader must paint a mental picture of the preferred outcome if people are going to grasp the vision. If the vision is not clear in the leader's mind, it becomes a thick fog bank in everyone else's.

Effective leaders never assume an idea is clear to others. Presume a certain degree of mental haze. Communication tools such as repetition, variety of message, and attention to message design are essential. Effective communication is not easy. It's an art.

Asking people to articulate what they perceive the vision to be can be a disconcerting but helpful practice. How many times do we talk to people and presume they understand what we are saying, only to discover that we were on completely different frequencies? Until proven otherwise, assume people do not have a clear signal.

Imagine conditions, circumstances, and emotions if we do not pursue and accomplish the vision. Establishing a worst-case scenario if we lose can be effective too because we presume things will continue as they have. A group's perceived need for change often begins with the fear of failure. A proper gloom report is not the end goal of a vision cast, but it may be the necessary soil preparation for people to respond to a solution. Far too often leaders try to sell solutions instead of problems. Adults rarely accept a solution to a problem they don't believe exists.

Good communicators start with the audience, not the message. Who are you trying to convince? Do they need to be dissuaded first? Are they negative, neutral, or mildly enthusiastic? The ability to read an audience is a prerequisite for good communication. Everyone listening has different motivations and something to gain or lose from the proposal. Talk to people to gather a sense of their direction, but don't rely on surveys to determine whether or not to pursue a dream. People who rely on surveys to establish visions are *not* leaders. They are wannabe influencers who coined the slogan, "If people lead, the leaders will follow." Vision begins in the minds of leaders but addresses the interests in followers and encourages them to action.

People need vision specifics. Everyone is motivated about something. Every leader must first believe people want to be inspired by the mandate, and then all they need is the opportunity to see, understand, and experience the vision in advance.

Shell 2: Always Answer the Questions *Why* and *When*

Why really means: Is it important? *When* really means: Is it urgent? *Importance* and *urgency* are the two most crucial issues in the life of a vision. In this age, with so many options available, we must be quick to respond to questions.

Visions cost something. They require time, energy, talent, and money. Meetings, tasks, communication, conflict management, and other resources are consumed by worthy visions. A dream that costs nothing is, for all practical purposes, useless, and it will rarely garner the commitment we desire.

People need to be reminded of the *why* of paying the

price and of the importance of investing their valuable time in pursuit of the vision. If we do not establish and reestablish the value of a vision, people will begin to devalue it. One of the most difficult tasks of any effective leader is to be redundant. Yes, redundant! Never assume people remember why they are doing what they're doing. The reason many people have lost their zeal, whether in work or in church, is because they have forgotten why they do what they do. Robotic business behaviors and mindless religious traditions reflect a lost sense of purpose.

Just because *you* deem something is important is not enough to motivate most people. *Urgency* is the accelerator. Most people would agree that exercise, proper eating, and doctor checkups are important. But only when you call 911 for chest pain, are rushed to the emergency room, and are told by the doctor, "The tests show that if you don't start exercising and eating right, you're going to meet your maker soon," are you apt to make some changes. Time is of the essence. If people can put on the back burner an important task for the sake of a more urgent matter, they will. Excellent leaders motivate followers with a sense of urgency and passion.

Why and *when* matters are the necessities of effective vision casting. History is full of examples of good leaders who could have been great had they been able to communicate the importance and urgency of a vision. If our vision is understood as important and urgent, then we can expect people to rise to the occasion—to interrupt their busy lives for the sake of the cause.

Shell 3: Do Not Be Afraid to Take a Calculated Risk

There are risk-takers and risk-reducers in this life. Risk-takers come in two types: groupers and non-groupers. Non-groupers are individualists who do everything by themselves, whether it's bungee jumping, day trading, or inventing. Groupers are leaders who take the risk of asking for help—leaders who understand the project is too big to achieve alone. Groupers want to share the excitement as well as the rewards of accomplishing the dream with a team.

Risk is the price tag of a dream; every vision requires an investment of time, money, and energy in order to tap into the latent potential around us. The word *potential* is like a new gold mine—it shows promise but is yet untried; has possibilities but must be pursued. "Some assembly required" is on the box of every vision. What most leaders fail to understand is that the accomplishment of the vision is anti-climactic. Hope is found in the pursuing of the dream created by the anticipation of something good. People need hope to live happily. Leaders are purveyors of hope. They manufacture hope by helping people see that something good will happen through teamwork.

Exceptional leaders are good melon thumpers. When seasoned fruit buyers examine a melon, they will thump it with their index finger. The sound of the thump lets the buyer know whether it's green, overly ripe, or just right. Leaders thump ideas and situations to see if they are ripe for investment—even when they cannot see any fruit yet. Upon finding a situation with potential, they gather people and resources to pursue the potential locked inside. This is done by communicating a vision of the preferred future. The leader describes the ripeness of the situation and helps potential followers see, smell, and taste the fruit even before it is in hand.

While most people look on the outside and have a difficult time seeing what can be, leaders are endowed with the gift of seeing what the future *could be*.

During his 1968 presidential campaign, Robert F. Kennedy remarked, "Some men look at things as they are and ask 'Why?' I look at things as they might be and ask 'Why not?'" Just as sculptors see the final work of art inside the block of marble and remove the extra to unleash it, leaders foresee the possibilities in a situation or idea and pursue them. To the non-leader, seeing is believing. To the leader, believing is seeing.

There is a direct proportion in the amount of risk taken and the amount of payoff possible. The banking system is a good illustration of this. The lowest risk, safest place to put your money is in a federally insured savings account. The higher the risk, the less safe is the money; but that kind of investment pays a higher dividend if successful. Very little in life is guaranteed. If you want to achieve much, you must take risks to gain the reward. The exception is when you reach the point of diminishing returns, when more investment quickly dissipates in unaltered productivity. Like pouring milk into an already full glass, excess will spill out and be lost. Remember, there is a fine line between being foolish and being full of faith.

Shell 4: Sacrifice in Order to Raise the Level of Commitment

Commitment opportunities are a dime a dozen these days. We are inundated with invitations to watch, read, or purchase things. When we feel overwhelmed with information, it's called information overload. We shut down and block out all further messages. In a similar fashion, when potential followers are overwhelmed with opportunities to participate in various projects and leadership situations, they can easily shut down due to overload.

What makes vision stand out among the rest of the messages going on around us? How can a leader emerge from a blurry field of others? Perhaps more than anything, people want to know how committed a leader is to a specific dream. They're questioning, *If this is such a great vision, are you willing to sacrifice for it? If you're asking me to expend my limited resources, what is your investment?* Leaders must be willing to consider the personal cost before they ask others to join them. When an escape route is clearly marked, and it's obvious the leader has few assets committed, it's almost impossible to empower a vision.

When the salesman sells Toyotas but drives a Honda, be suspicious. Nothing sells a blood drive better than seeing the leader donating blood. Like it or not, all leaders are in sales. They sell the intangibles of dreams and things to become. They deal in future options, recognizing that faith must be backed with personal sacrifice. Every potential buyer asks the same question, "What's in it for me?" If a leader is unable to answer this question effectively, there will be few purchasers of the dream.

When you hear a person say, "People just don't want to commit these days," chances are you are listening to an uncommitted leader. There is no such thing as an unmotivated person. We all make commitments in life, prioritizing what we deem is valuable. The leader's responsibility is to help others reprioritize their commitments and keep them motivated.

A GOOD LEADER CAN RAISE PEOPLE TO HEIGHTS THEY MAY HAVE ONLY IMAGINED IN DAYDREAMS AND CHILDHOOD ASPIRATIONS.

The single best way to get people to pursue the vision is for the leader to willingly sacrifice. The greatest motivational example of this was Jesus, whose crucifixion became the symbol for generations of followers. Just prior to the crucifixion, most of His disciples ran away in fear—one denying Him publicly three times. After the crucifixion, 11 of the 12 died as martyrs, resulting in a movement that spread to the entire world and has continued for centuries. Leaders must be willing to die for the vision if they are going to have the power to engage the commitment of others. Effective leaders continuously convey the importance and demonstrate the sort of sacrifice they desire.

Shell 5: Make the Connection to Emotions

Emotions are the front porch of the soul. That is why music and singing are an integral part of worship services. While emotion is at times misperceived as spirituality, rarely will we be moved spiritually without deeply stirred feelings. We are most apt to make spiritual commitments when we have been touched emotionally. Few make a connection with God on a purely intellectual basis.

Leading, like spirituality, needs to be fueled by passion. Touch the intellect, and you move part of the person; touch the soul, and you move the entire person. The soul represents the center of gravity of our personhood.

Each life shifts in emotion, action, and prioritization with the center.

Of the two primary tools of persuasion, *logos* (logic) and *pathos* (passion/emotion), the greatest by far is pathos. When communicating vision, utilize the five senses whenever possible. Visual aids, graphics, music, textures to touch, aromas to smell, and interactive environments to experience all lend themselves to dream catching. Leaders employ reminders that symbolize something intangible. Color, lighting, sound, and pictures communicate emotion.

Even the most left-brained, non-emotive person you know has soft spots: children, close friends, parents, memories, fond experiences, hobbies. Do not be intimidated by the pseudosophistication among the self-important. These are but smoke screens, protecting a heart that yearns for meaning, love, and purpose. Address the need for meaningful destiny and significance, both of which are basic to human nature. Leaders are about raising people to heights they may have only imagined in daydreams and childhood aspirations.

No matter how well you know the subject or how passionate you are about your dream, you must understand what motivates the people you lead. What's their hot button? What makes them laugh, cry, or get angry? What lights up their eyes? Addressing these issues and tying them to the vision are what trigger the emotion switch.

Leaders often overemphasize mass communication and underutilize dealing with influencers one-on-one. Leaders unwilling to sell the dream face-to-face will always leave leadership resources on the table. "Ask and it will be given to you" is a viable rule regarding leaders. To assume that people will initiate interest, volunteer from impersonal communication, and make commitments from broadcast advertisements is a shortcut to failure. Even in the world of social media, nothing beats the personal touch. People of influence are often inundated with messages to the masses. Never underestimate the timeless, risky practice of personally asking people to buy into the dream. Effective leaders appeal to the positive emotions of the people they lead.

4

THE LEADER'S METHOD

Learning to Help Your People Succeed

With his wife and kids honoring prior commitments, Tim found himself alone at the beach house for the weekend. He wanted to keep his next appointment with Paul, and the alone time gave him the opportunity to catch up on some planning and to contemplate the leadership lessons he was learning and striving to activate.

Before meeting with his mentor, Tim took a long walk. Finally arriving at the beach cottage, Tim yelled, "It's a great day, Paul!"

"Hello, my friend," Paul said with a friendly wave. "I see you're holding me to my word about our meetings."

"I don't want to miss a minute of our time together," Tim said, climbing the stairs from the sand to the deck where Paul waited. "Whenever I get here, you're already sitting outside. Do you spend a lot of time enjoying the ocean?"

"I've seen better health in my days. I enjoy the early mornings to converse with God and give thanks for the beauty of His creation. Learned that from a wise guy in Ecclesiastes, but I've had a hard time applying it until recently. Doctor says I need to slow down a bit and take pleasure in each hour as it comes."

"Are you okay?"

"Oh, just the normal growing-old stuff. The spirit is willing, but the flesh is weak."

For the first time, Tim was beginning to realize Paul's health might be failing. He rarely got out of his chair.

"Well, I'm game to learn about the third point of the star," Tim said. "I've been consciously working on putting more heart into my leading, as well as assessing my own motives and drive."

"That's great, Tim. Obviously, I can *introduce* you to the five key points in five weeks, but it's going to take you longer to implement them in your context and work environment. Because time is of the essence, let's look at the third main arena that separates exceptional leaders from wan-nabes." Paul looked at the large starfish hanging on the wall and continued, "The third area that frequently log-jams leadership is people. Leadership often gets hamstrung by relationships because people can often be a grind. The method you use to lead people is so important."

"That makes sense. How do leaders get out of sync with people, and how can that be prevented?"

"It's true that some people get out of sync in terms of their relationships with one another. The most prominent problems, though, have to do with a leader's basic people skills."

Tim looked up. "Help me understand this one more time. When you talk about reducing 80 percent of the most common problems within leadership, you're talking about leader problems as opposed to organizational matters."

"I'm afraid so. I'm not trying to imply that leaders are everything or that even superior leaders don't run into roadblocks and impossible complexities, but we're talking sheer percentages. What I've seen time after time is that leaders themselves clog the natural leadership development process when they fail to employ some basic people skills."

"I haven't met many leaders who are great with relation-ships," Tim said. "I mean, if they are too people oriented, it seems they don't get as much done."

"Old-school leadership might concur. Crisis management might agree. But for long-term effectiveness in these complex times, superior people skills are needed. The challenge of a leader is to stay evenly balanced between *being* and *doing*. If you are too people oriented, you'll never get to the work at hand, and you'll frustrate your more talented people who want to feel fulfilled by using their energies toward an intended outcome. On the other hand, if you load up too much on task, you'll alienate people."

"Seems to me that most leaders err in being too task driven," Tim offered.

"I agree."

"Specifically, what areas do I need to work on or look out for in my people orientation?"

"Well, a common hitch is in aligning people's strengths with organizational needs and roles. Never underestimate the importance of talent. Having willing people with good hearts is nice, but it doesn't guarantee tasks will be accomplished.

"The first step is to look at the talent pool and analyze the attitude, disposition, and experience you have available. Superior leaders are those who align people with places that match their strengths and minimize their weaknesses. Actually, that's what Peter Drucker, a well-known author and speaker about management and leadership, suggested as the main purpose of an organization. If you have great people in the wrong places, you'll clog up the organization. You can't solely rely on human resources, luck, or anyone else to carry the primary burden for this responsibility. Larger organizations have to delegate this task, but primary picks are always leader burdens."

"What else?"

"In step number two, leaders must provide time and a safe environment for people to process innovations. Because leaders are about change, they often misunderstand how people respond to change. Most people need adequate time and information to adjust to most change in life. When an organization incorporates improvements, however, many leaders misread the emotional response of their people with regard to change. They assume people have bad attitudes, are negative, or even are subversive to a leader's authority. Identifying the normal issues that arise when change is happening is healthy," Paul explained.

"I'm following you. I've encountered attitude problems at work. Recently, we've been going through significant changes, and I have been frustrated with people who didn't seem to catch on to what we are doing. Looking back, I believe I may have alienated some of my people."

"It can happen if we forget to love our people as much as our work. The truth is, we need as many as possible rowing in the same direction in order to get the job done."

"That is a great analogy. Tell me more."

"A leader's ability to confront will either make or break what the leader is trying to accomplish. Leaders who are afraid to confront actually damage the organization by allowing mediocre performance. The end result is that it demotivates the other team members, which, in turn, hurts productivity. You can't let below average or modest performance and attitudes continue for any length of time. If you need a lot of affirmation, you'd better surrender your role as leader. Of course, pretending you don't need people and enjoying your confrontational role too much is just as unhealthy. Some leaders seem to take pleasure in intimidating people. Good communication skills bring the right balance and greatly enhance one's confrontational abilities."

"I don't like confronting," Tim said. "Sometimes, I lie awake at night when I know that the next morning I have to deal with someone at the office."

"That's good, Tim. That probably means you are doing it better than most. Wrestling with the need to confront has a positive way of refining the motives, words, and attitude of the leader. But you can't allow people to be lazy or sloppy. When you confront honestly with compassion, people appreciate you more. When people are fearful, hurt, and angry, they will inevitably hinder leadership."

"You're saying leadership is reduced when the leader fails to effectively confront."

"Absolutely."

"But what about the times when you don't have to confront? Besides the talent issue, what people skills are needed to enhance the flow of leadership?"

"Let me toss in a third step that might answer your question. Exceptional leaders are unique in that they have the ability to love people and encourage them to feel good about themselves and the organization. The best leaders are excellent lovers, you might say."

"Whew, maybe I should tell my wife," Tim said smiling.

Paul chuckled. "You know what I mean. Just because you're a leader doesn't make you any more or less a human being. The same is true of followers. When leaders fail to understand that the motivating desire of every worker is self-esteem, the leader inevitably hampers the main goal, which is leading."

"But many organizations are far away from implementing this value. How do they get things done?"

"Not easily. Look at their turnover. Examine the high cost of recruiting, training, and finding substitutes for sick leave as well as the reduced productivity of people who do not feel loved, respected, and valued. I like the term you used, 'value,' because that's what we're talking about. Our God-given value is at the core of who we are and what we desire in life. When leaders treat people like performers or boxes on a flowchart, productivity shuts down. Superior leaders understand the importance of affirmation, listening, esteem, and basic love."

"I guess you never get too old for love, do you?"

"No, never, Tim. Not even at my age. People skills are the equivalent to the transmission in a car. Without them, you don't get very far, even if you have a steering wheel and an engine. Through developing and maintaining positive relationships, you greatly enhance the natural flow of leadership. Leaders set the pace. They model what is and isn't important to an organization. People are the most important part of every organization."

The two men talked until noon and then parted company. Tim glowed from his new discoveries about leadership methods. Full of ideas and with his mind racing with ways to implement his ideas, he returned to his house along the beach.

SHELLS FROM THE MENTOR'S BASKET

Shell 1: Deal with Conflict as It Arises

Leaders understand that their primary enemy is disunity, not differences. Effective leaders neither welcome nor run from conflict. They respond to it appropriately as the need arises. Conflict is a celebration of the human spirit—the diversity of perceptions, experiences, gifts, and free will. So long as conflict can add to better understanding, heightened commitment, greater communication—thus problem solving—it should be embraced. Avoiding conflict in order to muffle any communication that isn't in complete agreement with you and ostracizing messengers bearing bad news are signs of unhealthy leadership.

To enjoy conflict is neurotic. To hate it to the point of avoiding it at all costs is pathological in the other direction. Good leaders know the balance.

The reason we dread conflict is because we have heard about dismal outcomes. Like the Pavlovian response of a mistreated dog that flinches at the mere raising of a hand, people with negative conflict experiences wince at anything reflecting differences of opinion. Think about the following four ways to deal with conflict:

1. *Use excellent communication to avoid conflict.* The root of many differences of opinion is a lack of information. Making sure team members, especially decision makers, are kept in the loop is an important means of avoiding unnecessary conflicts. Team building—where people interact for community, relationship building, and even fun—goes a long way in avoiding tension points.

2. *Welcome the messenger of conflict.* People who deliver

less than positive messages should be esteemed and affirmed for their willingness to get involved. When leaders reject a person raising a conflict issue, they give the appearance of being closed minded. This reflects poorly on the leader, and perception is vital to influence.

3. *Never allow conflict to smolder.* People will not approach a leader if they feel intimidated. Therefore, it's the leader's responsibility to initiate contact with those in conflict. To confront an organizational matter is what leaders are supposed to do. While you should not micromanage, you also should not let a small sliver become a big infection. Behave like an organizational doctor and address the situation.

4. *Respond to conflict appropriately.* You should not shoot a fly with a bazooka, but neither should you place a Band-Aid on a life-threatening wound. Confront one-on-one. Listen. Ask questions. Withhold judgment. Request suggestions from the parties involved. Should you come to an impasse, include others in the process. Express appreciation to the person, and always be gracious.

Shell 2: Let Your Servanthood Shine Through

Leaders are in the people business. Were it not for people, leadership would not exist. Effective leaders do not think of themselves as CEOs, superiors, presidents, or chairpersons. Instead, they foster the image of a servant. They exist to help others. In the context of leadership, the tool for serving may not be a towel and basin, but rather the gift of influence. The ability to unify leadership is unique and is vital to the success of an organization. Churches, businesses, and communities needing to experience change require leaders who will assist people in their journey to vision fulfillment.

"What can I do for you?" "What resources do you need to utilize your talents?" "How can I help you maximize your potential?" These are the kinds of questions servant leaders ask of their people. Non-servant leaders tend to ask the same questions in reverse, "What can you do for me?" "What do I need from you to help me use my talents?" "How can you help me maximize my potential?" Many people join an organization with a "What's in it for me?" attitude. For some it's a paycheck, but for most it has more to do with a sense of camaraderie, fulfillment, and self-expression. These people don't exist for the leader's benefit. The leader's job is to serve them so that they, in turn, can serve the organization. In other words, you are at the bottom of the totem pole. Because the leader's role is so vital to the health and well-being of the organization, most receive larger proportions of resources, such as power, salary, and freedom. You reap what you sow. With responsibility comes reward.

This inverse attitude of thinking like a servant has the tendency to endear a leader to people in any organization. Endearing leaders, unlike most, have the ability to gain exceptional trust, appreciation, and commitment from those involved in the organization. Humility and approachability are greatly esteemed qualities among leaders. Residual negative experiences with past authority figures create an unconscious fear and resentment factor in most people. When leaders portray the spirit of service, they diminish these relational toxins. The win-win attitude creates a leadership atmosphere that increases participant tenure, commitment, and enjoyment.

Effective leaders think of themselves as servants more than as leaders. While their method is to utilize people, servant leaders are not people users. When led properly, people do not feel manipulated or exploited. In fact, even in disagreements, followers understand a servant leader's heart to do what is best for the organization.

Shell 3: Help People Find Places Where They Can Succeed

If people are the primary assets of any organization, then talents are the building blocks of those assets.

Sit in the lobby of a first-class hotel, and you will experience a multitude of talents coming together for a sublime experience. Flower farmers grow beautiful blooms so that a professional arranger can put them together in a lovely bouquet to grace the center of the lobby. This bouquet is placed on a large, marble-topped table held up by ornate metalwork. The marble was expertly excavated from a mine in Italy and then cut and polished by craftsmen. Metal artisans creatively put their talents into the base to finish the classy furnishing. Other artists etched floral designs in the huge front windows and the door glass of the entrance. Woodcrafters and builders, along with architectural designers, created an open, artistic main entrance. Bellmen devote their attention to people details—getting the doors for residents, helping them with their bags, parking their cars. The concierge uses knowledge of the local area to answer questions of guests. The chef in the restaurant prepares delicious food that is provided by a friendly waiter to the tables. Lighting technicians, computer experts, interior designers, construction workers, financiers, carpet makers and layers, tile manufacturers, maintenance people, and managers use their talents and skills together to make one tiny section of the universe a delightful experience. This cooperation is a microcosm of any effective organization. No one could do it alone. All can do it together, using their unique talents.

An organizational guru once said that the purpose of an organization is to maximize people's strengths and minimize their weaknesses. In order for this to occur, effective leaders employ the ABCs of leadership:

Analyze the assets of the organization. Before connecting people with positions, the leader must understand what kind of talent is needed to improve the organization. A great leader surveys the organization and its assets and then recruits the necessary talent.

Become people focused. Study the strengths of your personnel. What do they do well? What do they naturally do better than most? The answers to these questions reflect areas where they will enjoy participation, bringing both skill and attitude assets. Do not worry about improving weaknesses unless they steal from their strengths.

Connect talent with obvious needs. Talented people placed properly will bring about organizational success. The excellent leader searches for talented employees and matches their talent with the needs of the organization.

Shell 4: Make Goal Achievement Enjoyable

Enjoyable? The word smacks of kids playing on jungle gyms at recess, not of adults pursuing serious organizational goals. What does *enjoyable* have to do with achievement? Pretty soon you'll start using the word *fun*. Similar thoughts may go through the minds of typical leaders, but atypical leaders—the ones who are loved and who are also productive—learn the secret element of success: making organizational life enjoyable. Effective leaders take fun seriously. This includes the use of appropriate humor, laughter in meetings, team building in and out of the office, personal notes, personalized gifts, spontaneous activities, and courteous frivolity. Team leaders, like parents, sometimes have a difficult time knowing how much levity to induce into a team. Some members are already predisposed to make work or ministry into a leisure activity, just as others are prone to segregate work from any form of fun.

With so many work and time options available, exceptional leaders should accentuate the amenities of serving under their supervision. By intentionally cultivating an atmosphere where goal achievement is enjoyable, they provide intangible benefits that supersede mere monetary ones. Here are a few examples:

- *Community building:* Community is all but lost in twenty-first-century American society. Due to mobility, corporate mergers and takeovers, depletion of the nuclear family, brain drain within smaller towns, and cross-cultural realities, people today are experiencing mass loneliness. By intentionally creating community within a team, the leader increases

BY INTENTIONALLY CULTIVATING AN ATMOSPHERE WHERE GOAL ACHIEVEMENT IS ENJOYABLE, LEADERS PROVIDE INTANGIBLE BENEFITS THAT SUPERSEDE MERE MONETARY ONES.

communication possibilities. Community building comes via sharing personal anecdotes at meetings, scheduling nonwork socials, and scheduling off-site retreats that include relationship building.

- *Monotony breakers:* Hire someone to come in to do five-minute back/shoulder massages. Take the staff for a cup of coffee or for a catered picnic lunch at a nearby park. Interrupt work to tell a funny story. These are means of reducing tension, revitalizing energy, and creating an atmosphere where people wonder, *What's going to happen next?* Curiosity extends attention. Anticipation increases hope. These emotional endorphins catalyze joy in goal achievement.

- *Spontaneous creativity training:* Watching a film clip, discussing an intriguing current event, or reading an inspirational selection—which may or may not have anything to do with the meeting agenda itself—are ways to engage interaction and awaken imagination. Providing practical lessons and creating group discussion can create joy amidst potentially mundane situations, not to mention the redeeming value of continuing education. The key is making sure there is a bridge to how this may relate to the productivity. Learning and growing are rewarding activities people appreciate.

- *Use a little humor:* Nothing can engage or alienate people as quickly as humor. The best leaders laugh at themselves. Laughing at someone else's expense and introducing sexual and ethnic comedy are alienators. The consistent use of smiles, laughter, wholesome jokes, cartoons, and silly articles are wonderful ways to crack a smile and decorate a work environment with joy. Lighten up. Even during the most stressful meetings and projects, appropriate humor will significantly improve attitudes.

Shell 5: Take Good Care of the Team

Are you people oriented or task oriented? Everyone has a preference. High achievers tend to be task oriented because they focus on the work at hand. The best leaders tend to be 60 to 70 percent task oriented but know how and when to focus on people. The weakness of many leaders is an overemphasis on task.

Superior leaders have an array of people skills in their

toolbox. It's important in an enduring task-oriented organization to implement a superior people orientation. The paramount need is to care for people as individuals. Every employee is more than just his or her job. Considering the complexity of the people you lead is essential in conveying your care for them. Do you know a basic history of those in your sphere of influence? Do you know the names of their spouses, children, and close friends? What are their hot buttons, pet peeves, weaknesses, and strengths? What are their significant dates: birthday, anniversary, loss of a parent, divorce, or joining the organization?

Each person has a variety of windows into his or her life. Knowing what these are allows a leader to make significant headway into knowing that person. Sending a card, a personal note, an individualized reward, or thoughtful email are vehicles to convey care. Picking up a soccer magazine at the grocery store because a team member's son loves the sport, passing on a complimentary email, and leaving a smiley face sticky note are all means of saying "I care." The most effective and perhaps most taxing leadership skill is that of listening. For the task-oriented person, there is a strong, albeit unconscious, sense that spending time listening is an ineffective and wasted activity. Task-oriented people are doers. They conduct meetings if it's important to accomplishment but rarely as a caring activity. That is why leaders who are overly task oriented often create leadership environments that are known to use people. Even though these leaders are known as productive, company turnover and criticism run high.

Ask people to think of leaders they know who have significantly impacted their lives, and chances are you will hear stories of those who communicated care. Effective leaders go beyond the call of duty by employing methods such as sending flowers for a personal loss or celebration and providing time off during a difficult time. Such daily interactions are ways to genuinely say, "I care for you as a person."

5

THE LEADER'S MODEL

Learning How to Get
Integrity from Your People

The next Saturday, as Tim climbed the stairs to Paul's deck, he noticed Paul walking slowly toward his chair and then wincing as he sat down.

"Are you okay, Paul?"

"Oh, just the pain of a full season of living. I can't complain," Paul said with a sigh and a smile. "It's good to see you, Tim. How did your week go?"

"It was pretty full. I've spent a lot of between-meeting and before-bedtime moments going over the principles we discussed last week. Your ideas are changing the way I think about leadership. Funny, my wife says she can see a difference in the way I treat her and the kids."

"That happens. Effective leaders are more effective in all they do, not just leading. It has a lot to do with maturity. People who are task driven without love can make money and gain recognition, but most folks don't like to be around them."

"I'm discovering that leading well has a lot to do with getting beyond myself."

"That's good. Superior leading is really about service, isn't it? When people enjoy following your leadership, you know you are doing it right. Are we ready to unpack the fourth point of the star?" Paul asked, pointing toward the starfish on the sun-bleached cottage wall.

As the sunlight pierced the morning dawn, Tim pulled out his tablet. "We're good to go."

"Great. The fourth point has to do with a strategic area where leadership often gets hung up. It's the character of the leader. The character of a leader is equivalent to the materials of a vehicle, whether you make it out of tin, plastic, steel, alloy, or fiberglass. When you use cheap materials, you'll get a car that falls apart in a short time. Every follower needs a solid leadership model."

"Sounds like the fable of the three little pigs. You know: the straw, stick, and brick houses."

"That's good. In that analogy, the big bad wolf might be difficult decisions, peer pressure, temptation, or any of a number of stress factors. Stress tends to reveal character. Who you are when no one is looking will affect the way you lead."

"Yet character seems kind of old fashioned and passé," Tim said. "I mean, recent political leaders' escapades didn't seem to take away from their popularity. Why is character an important issue?"

"Character is who you are, not just what you do. Leaders are social artists. Their influence transcends what they do and how they solve problems. Their actions and attitudes influence and model leadership."

"Can you give me some examples?"

"Sure. What makes you think that a person, any person, who adopts one value system at home will significantly change those values when in public or in a work environment? Would you hire someone you knew had stolen from his parents, cheated on his wife, and yelled at his kids? What makes you think that person would be honest, committed, and relational at work?"

"He might be because the conditions are different?"

"Perhaps, but probably not. Given the right conditions, that person is apt to resort to his core value system, good or bad. I grew up on a farm in the Midwest where there were cattle paths. The paths were often not straight but curved unpredictably through the grass and weeds to a water hole. While these paths were not direct, the cows preferred them because they were familiar, worn, and unencumbered. The moral and ethical decisions we make reflect our character. They are equivalent to the cow paths. We resort to these patterns because they are familiar or habitual. You cannot separate a leader from his character if you are to assume predictable behavior. Followers place their trust in a leader who models integrity."

"Where do you think a leader's character hinders leadership most often?"

"I believe the most common is compromising in order to achieve. Because the ultimate goal of leadership is some sort of group task accomplishment, leaders with character issues will tend to take shortcuts and pursue questionable solutions if they're expedient. While short-term gains can be had, enduring leadership requires the moral and ethical high road. You can look at history if you want proof."

"You're saying nice guys finish first."

"I'm saying people of character finish best. When you compromise here and there in terms of values, morals, and ethics, you run the risk of losing the respect of those who follow you, and you endanger the outcome. Our creator designed us to function according to certain enduring principles, many of which have to do with our character."

"So why is a leader's character more important than a follower's?"

"Primarily because leaders influence those who follow and usually make more and broader decisions, which impact the whole process. Influence is akin to an amplifier that increases the perceptions of who we are. Small character defects become more pronounced when we are placed in leadership positions."

"But what if you don't want the pressure of being a role model for others?"

"Then don't become a leader! Society needs role models. That is how each generation learns how to behave. If we do not provide an example others should model, we should voluntarily resign roles we have as leaders."

"I'm not sure if I like that kind of pressure to perform. I don't feel comfortable with the idea that my team is watching me in terms of my character," Tim admitted.

"Well, they are. An organization tends to become like its leader. If you are loving, there will be love within the ranks. If you are honest, dishonesty will not be tolerated. If you are lazy, team members won't work hard. If you cut corners and look the other way when indiscretions occur, your followers will probably do the same."

"Have you ever met a perfect role model?"

"Character and perfection are different matters, Tim. Character is about striving for the high road. It's equally about admitting and recognizing our imperfections and yet not using them to excuse our behaviors. Character is about humility and repentance when necessary."

"Why is it so many leaders who do so much good end up going wrong? Why are there so many crash-and-burn stories out there?"

"Pressure reveals flaws, defects, and cracks in our character. When leaders don't maintain substantial moral margins, they are apt to make poor choices when stressed. Leaders need policies and people who will keep them from facing compromising choices alone. Maintaining fences between neighbors is a good idea. It keeps cows out of their corn and dogs from biting their children. Sexual affairs, inappropriate talk, deception, and under-the-table deals hamstring leaders left and right. When you avoid accountability, pursue unwholesome alliances, and fail to nurture your value system, you are headed for a fall."

"Do you think leaders are more or less prone to character defects?"

"I think many leaders have high character because it's an important part of leadership. Without strong character, leaders can easily disqualify themselves for the role. But at the same time, power and influence tend to make us believe we are invincible—that we don't need to be held accountable. This kind of narcissistic belief is a definite liability for those who lead. Character dangers within leading are real, which is why leaders should pursue their roles with respect and a healthy degree of trepidation."

"Why does the character of the leader hinder leadership?"

"As you can see, we keep going back to the same principle. Leadership is a natural social process that wants to happen. But to remove the logjams, we need to focus our attention on leader issues more than organizational matters. When a person lacking in character is setting policy, making people decisions, and serving as an organizational role model, these character flaws will hinder leadership from happening as it should. People inside the organization will tend to withhold trust and/or replicate what they see. People outside the organization will avoid strong alliances and question doing business with such an entity."

"Okay, so what about well-known leaders who were notorious for being womanizers or brutal bosses? Why did their character flaws not hinder their leading?"

"In many cases, when you take a closer look at their lives, you'll discover problems created by these character issues. We must also admit to the complexities of leadership. Sometimes mediocre people succeed simply because they find themselves in the right place at the right time. Their success has more to do with luck than ability. I'd speculate that some leaders are effective in spite of their character flaws, not because of them." Paul paused a moment, and then he said, "I wonder what these same people might have accomplished had they been people of strong character."

Tim stood up, stretched, and shook hands with his white-haired mentor. After saying goodbye, he started down the beach toward his cottage. He stopped to pick up trash from the beach and then talked out loud to himself about becoming a good leadership model for his coworkers.

SHELLS FROM THE MENTOR'S BASKET

Shell 1: Establish an Accountability Flow

Effective leaders know weak points exist in all organizations and people. Therefore, they take conscientious actions to fortify those flawed places by arranging accountability safeguards.

Superior leaders seek to surround themselves with an accountability system that helps them avoid character failure. This practice in and of itself is a sign of strength versus weakness. A major character flaw is to believe oneself to be above failure and immune to the temptations other leaders face. Here are three common systems that can provide accountable safety boundaries:

1. *Peers:* Leaders are often lonely because they are unable to share many of their challenges with anyone else in their organization. Intentionally seeking out peers, professionals from other organizations, or people in a church or Bible study group is a way to stay grounded. Reciprocal accountability is essential.

2. *Practices:* Establish rules and standards that are both moral and ethical—ideals that help organizational members to avoid trouble. Set clear standards for accountability of time, money, behavior with the opposite sex, travel, and meeting protocol. These rules should apply to the actions of the leader as well as anyone else on the team. Establish structures that provide appropriate reward and penalty.

3. *Feedback:* Many leaders fail when they ignore input from staff, customers, or team members. Spending time listening to good feedback can reduce exposure to temptations that have befallen many leaders. By surrounding oneself with yes people or those who stand to lose by raising accountability questions, leaders often sabotage themselves and the organizations they lead.

Shell 2: Establish Personal Values and Beliefs

Leaders respond to morally gray areas best when they have preestablished their value system. One popular belief system assumes everything is relative; that truth does not exist, and situations determine one's response. This is unreliable and risky for someone whose decisions influence other people. Leaders need to concentrate on establishing a personal standard for living.

In a world where converging values create daily conflict, it's crucial for strong leaders to be clear on what they believe. Internal stress will be greatly reduced if predetermined values of what you will and will not do are bolted down in advance of the storm. Nurturing values is important because unattended character, like raw dirt, tends to erode with the elements of time. Studying the Bible, meditating, and being in fellowship with people who have good morals will foster strong character.

People tend to reflect the character of their leaders. They rarely rise above the leader's morality and ethics. Leaders influence policy, reflect values, and provide a model for others. Who you are will determine what you do.

Excellent leaders realize it's their responsibility to make sure that values and beliefs are put into practice within the organization.

While it's true that a leader cannot impose personal

standards on the people within their organization, they must understand the importance of establishing dos and don'ts based on moral and spiritual values.

Shell 3: Always Take the High Road

Leaders must read moral road maps. They look for landmarks that keep them on the ethical high road. This is an imperative for all leaders because they establish the moral climate of their organizations. If you want to get the caboose to the station, the engine must go past the train platform. What may be okay for others is not okay for you. An organization will not rise above the character model of its leaders. People emulate what they see. Exceptional leaders behave differently.

Moral chameleons change their colors to fit the situation. Self-esteem, reputation, and sense of pride will dissipate with every character compromise. Leaders without strong moral codes are eventually left to the side. Exceptions exist, where followers endure a less-than-wholesome leader in exchange for rewards, but effective leaders practice what they preach.

If in doubt, take the high road. Give people your best; treat people with class. Always be kind, and go for what is right more than what is expedient or profitable. The ends do not always justify the means. "What good is it for someone to gain the whole world, and yet lose or forfeit their very self?" (Luke 9:25).

To take the high road, superior leaders adopt a code of ethics. The Bible is the highest standard for making decisions that have moral and ethical implications. The ability to know and draw upon this godly wisdom requires tenacity. Peers, subordinates, and superiors may make fun of it, try to influence against it, and urge you to pursue compromise; but don't do it. Do what's right. Swim upstream!

Shell 4: Do Not Be Proud of Your Humility

When you begin to believe your own press releases, you are in trouble. Perhaps the greatest single danger a leader faces regarding character comes in the area of pride, which attacks our moral immune system. Leaders are dealers in power. "Powerless leader" is an oxymoron. Unfortunately, craving power is at the root of most human evil. It makes or breaks people. Power is an infectious virus, seeking to infiltrate any weak point in our character. Scripture says that "the love of money is a root of all kinds of evil" (1 Timothy 6:10), but money is merely a power resource.

Imagine power as a radioactive isotope, able to invisibly invade the life of anyone who comes into contact with it. Just as a nuclear engineer wears safety equipment, effective leaders don protective actions and attitudes that reduce the

"POWERLESS LEADER" IS AN OXYMORON.

risk of ego contamination. Consider the following three ways to remain humble:

1. *Keep your perspectives healthy.* The naked emperor was duped to believe that his royal blood allowed him to see clothes that were invisible to others. As he walked through the streets in his skivvies (or less), no one but an innocent child said anything for fear of being punished. When we punish those who question our decisions, bring negative feedback, or hold us accountable, we are putting on the "emperor's new clothes."

2. *Maintain a spirit of meekness.* By meekness, we do not mean a melancholy, pessimistic attitude. This meekness, or brokenness, reflects the taming of the soul. Humus is fertile soil that has been enriched by decaying living things. When we die to our own selfish ambitions, our souls become enriched. The manure that happens through the course of life and leading should not be thrown away because it is valuable as fertilizer. Humility is a sign of an enriched heart. When we allow naysayers, struggles, and failures to keep us humble, we avoid the danger of success going to our heads.

3. *Nurture an attitude of gratitude.* Effective leaders understand the importance of saying thanks on a continual basis. The words *thanksgiving* and *grace* are in the same Greek word family. To say grace before a meal is to thank

God for providing food to eat. People who recognize their need for grace tend to be gracious people. Leaders are most vulnerable to pride when they forget where they have come from and how they arrived at the door of success. Do not be like the man who was honored in a small town for his humility. The whole town turned out to celebrate a day in his honor. He was given a badge that read "Most Humble Man in Town." Unfortunately, when he started wearing the badge every day, they took it away from him!

Like a turtle on top of a fence post, exceptional leaders remember and appreciate those who helped them on the way to the top.

Shell 5: Persevere Until the End

Instant character can't be cooked up in a microwave. All leaders must take responsibility for who they are from the inside out. The challenges of leading make leaders either tender or brittle over time, depending on how they react to problems.

Study the lives of great leaders, and you will find something most have in common: They have overcome insurmountable problems in life. Whether they have faced health issues, childhood struggles, betrayals, setbacks, or organizational defeats, every effective leader has been an overcomer. Excellent leaders never run from the opportunity to grow. Remember, the tests of life season your concrete and strengthen your mettle.

Leaders grow through personal challenge. When we are broken in the right place, our souls are transformed. We mature, becoming wiser and more confident. When we respond poorly to times of brokenness, we become bitter, defeated, and angry people. The world is full of wounded people who gave up without growing from adversity.

Good character is manufactured during the tough times of life. When problems come, do not curse them—bless them! Don't rehearse your wound in order to gain pity from others and excuse a bad attitude. Rather, reverse your wound. Allow it to make you into a person who understands pain. Superior leaders are overcomers—they persevere to the very end!

6

THE LEADER'S MISSION

Learning How to Lead as a Whole Person

Tim's job was changing because he had begun to apply what he had discovered from his talks with Paul. On this Saturday morning, the coastal fog was thick, but the air was warm. As Tim headed to his meeting, he sipped his coffee and reminisced about the previous weeks of Saturday mornings with his newfound friend. Each meeting seemed to be a heaven-sent appointment, and the unhurried discussions provided opportunity to gather feedback and share dreams. As Tim approached Paul's house, he caught a glimpse of his mentor.

Surprisingly, Paul was standing at the railing of his deck. "Hello and good morning, my young friend. How has your week gone?"

"It's been great!" Tim exclaimed. Bounding up the stairs, he said, "You're looking chipper today."

"I'm moving a little slowly, but I feel pretty strong. It's easy to thank God for good days at my age. Have a seat, Tim, and let's get started. Speaking of legs, the Lord made the starfish with five of them, which means we only have one more area to discuss concerning effective leading." With the ocean roaring in the background, the men glanced at the starfish on the cottage wall one last time.

"I've been enjoying these talks so much, Paul, that I'm tempted to graft in another appendage or two."

Paul chuckled. "I've enjoyed our times as well. It's an honor to be asked to invest in the life of another person, especially one with the gift of leading. You see, your investment has the potential of paying off in large proportions."

"The honor is mine. I can't tell you how much I've learned from you this last month. I know I could never afford the professional coaching you've given me. Thanks so much."

"Mutual honor results when two people respectfully serve each other. I've served you with the wisdom I've gleaned after years of leading. And you've served me by listening and applying what you've learned. Life is too short to be less than humble, and too long to be less than gracious. Someone once said that a contented man does not measure the good that has been done to him but the good that he has done. Let's talk about the fifth area of leading."

"I'll admit I've been curious to know what that area is."

"Well, the fifth area where leaders hang up in the leadership process hasn't received much attention in the past. It has to do with the soul of the leader."

Tim stopped taking notes and looked up. "What did you say?"

"I said that the fifth point of that starfish represents the leader's soul. Twenty-first-century leading is returning to the realization that everyone is physical, mental, social, and spiritual. Many leaders now acknowledge the presence and power of God in our universe."

"How does a leader's soul interfere with leadership, Paul? I've always thought a person should separate his spiritual self from his public self. That's what most people seem to do."

"I know what you mean, but it's just not possible, considering that our spiritual core influences everything we do. Spirituality is like fuel to the automobile. The soul is the power that energizes the leader. If leaders are influential in empowering and guiding others, how important do you think it is that a leader learn to be able to discern between godly and human influences?"

"How does a lack of spirituality hinder the leadership process?"

"When you rely solely on human wisdom, personal power, and discernment, you are inhibiting your potential for leading. This, in turn, detracts from the capacity of the leadership process."

"Where do leaders fail the most in terms of spirituality?"

"Very simply stated, leaders fail when they ignore their need for supernatural empowerment."

"What causes us to ignore God?"

Paul paused before he responded. "As I stated previously, leaders are dealers in power. According to the Word of God, the downfall of humanity came when people pursued power. People seem to want to control their lives. It's been a shortcoming ever since Adam and Eve."

"How do leaders fall into this trap?"

"Leaders are human. They tend to operate within their own power. A power-crazed leader will lead people astray. In the pursuit of power, he or she forgets the soul. Therefore, the leader's first mission is taking care of his or her own soul."

Tim leaned back in his chair and said, "But if I do not separate my personal spirituality from my leading, won't people think of me more as a priest or a pastor? I'm a leader to lead, not preach."

"Tim, if you ever divorce what you do from your soul, then your spirituality doesn't amount to much, does it? People will understand who you are by how you communicate your mission. If you lead with God's guidance and power in your life, whether you're a president, pastor, politician, or corporate executive, people will recognize the difference."

"But I keep going back to all the people in history who seemed to have little sense of God or, at least, did not comply with His ways, yet they were revered as great leaders. What difference does it really make?"

"The fact that people have been great leaders without God is not a premise for godless leading. When you separate leading from the soul, you end up relying on human values versus the ageless truths regarding God's power and guidance. Our value system is vital to how and where we lead. Throughout history, leaders with corrupt, self-centered, and ungodly values have caused immeasurable pain and suffering to humanity. People are too precious to be placed in the hands of leaders who rely solely on their own wisdom, motives, and power. Life is too valuable to be handled poorly. The gift you've received needs to be handled responsibly."

"Where does a leader go for this kind of wisdom?"

"Everyone must have a place to go to gain the values by which he or she lives. I've found that the most dependable ones are explained in the Bible. Don't expect the wisdom of God's Word to work if you edit it or water it down. Take it as a whole and use it. Time has a way of proving truths, and the Bible is the best-tested spiritual guide in history. But there's another main reason why a leader needs to be in touch with his soul, as well as plugged in to the all-powerful, all-wise God."

"What's that?"

"The people you lead have souls as well. They are God's sheep, like you, lost or found. They have the image of their all-loving creator, regardless of any beliefs or actions they portray. People cannot ignore their need for spirituality. It impacts their values, motivations, decision making, and attitudes. The beauty of twenty-first-century leading is that we are experiencing a second Renaissance, an awakening of our spiritual side. You don't think that God would give you gifts and opportunities to impact the lives of people without touching their souls, do you? Eternity is written into all of us. As a leader, you have a unique ability to influence people. You must not waste the opportunity to merge your faith with your leading.

Tim laughed nervously. "I've never really taken the spiritual side of life seriously as a leader. The way you explain it makes so much sense, Paul. How do I apply what you're telling me? What should I do to become more spiritual in my leading?"

"Because our relationship with God is not a cookbook recipe, it's probably not wise to think of it in terms of a how-to list. Perhaps the most important point is to understand your motivation. Do you come to God in obedience or for some selfish motive? Next, pursue God's power. You can't possibly utilize power that you don't possess. When you limit God to a mere religious practice or set of beliefs, you render sterile His place in your life. You will need to spend time with Him in prayer. Read the Bible. And ask those who understand and live by it to help you in your spiritual journey. We need one another, and, most of all, God Himself, to achieve vibrant spirituality."

"I used to go to church for my wife and kids because I thought it was good for me personally. I never really considered how it might impact my leading."

"Most leaders don't understand its importance. That's why there are so few leaders who endure over the long haul. Very few finish without a crash-and-burn story. The role of God in your life is not just a church-oriented segment. He has the ability to transform the way you lead. Jesus used His divine power to literally transform civilization. His marvelous power source is available to help people like us do far more than we could ever accomplish by our own devices, no matter how dedicated, smart, or talented we might be."

"I'm going to make it my mission to take care of my soul. It's obvious I haven't scratched the surface on becoming the leader God wants me to be. I'm sure my lack of spirituality has slowed my leadership in many areas. I plan to change my ways immediately."

A sense of finality overwhelmed Tim as he gave Paul a hug and said farewell. Somehow Tim sensed this would be his last leadership lesson from his mentor. Later that night, while seated on the deck of their beach house, Tim shared his new insights about leadership with his wife. With a full moon glistening in the background, Tim gently took her hand and prayed a prayer asking God's help to turn his back on his selfish goals and to pursue whatever God had for him instead. He committed to make it his mission to always take care of his soul.

SHELLS FROM THE MENTOR'S BASKET

Shell 1: Watch Over Your Soul

At the core of every person is a spiritual soul. This epicenter represents the middle of our personage, influencing our values, relational skills, attitudes, actions, and decision making. When leaders take care of their soul, they become spiritually authentic. When transformed people lead, chances significantly increase for them to bring about transformation in people and organizations.

Effective leaders must lead in four directions: downward, upward, lateral, and inward. While most leadership books focus on downward leading—overseeing those below you in the organizational flowchart—that is only a small percentage of leadership effectiveness. Just as important is upward leading. Listening, responding to, and influencing superiors is important too, whether through reports, board members, powerful staff members, or stockholders. Lateral leading has to do with negotiating with peers, fellow team members, and organizational equals. Vying for resources and working together requires political savvy, but effective leaders also understand the need to go inward and watch over their souls. When a leader fails to take care of the spiritual, the entire organization will feel the ill effects.

Making the soul our first mission is essential to becoming a resource for others. Physical, mental, emotional, and spiritual dimensions are each vital to the developing of the whole person. If you are hollow spiritually, it will become evident in your leading. You will lack the inner power, peace, and guidance only God can bring, not to mention divine wisdom that surpasses mortal smarts. Stories abound of great men and women who relied solely on their own abilities, only to become sidetracked and manipulated by others and by their own skewed perceptions. Perhaps most importantly for a leader, keeping your soul centered on God provides a healthy perspective. Spiritual development is about maximizing all the potential that is available to humankind, including that which transcends mere humanity.

Taking time to study Scripture and to meditate and set aside moments for solitude are all vital regimens for effective leading. You cannot reach your potential with a shriveled soul. Feeding, exercising, and nurturing your own spiritual life enables you to do the same for others. Sometimes it's overt and occasionally it's covert, but you always bring spiritual wisdom and energy into the decisions, meetings, and daily interactions within your organization. People will notice. They will sense something different about the way you lead from those who rely solely on a keen mind or a quick wit. Some may think it is because you "got religion," but religion often lacks spiritual authenticity and power. Genuine soul growth has to do with developing a personal relationship with Jesus Christ.

Shell 2: Follow the Jesus Model and Join a Small Group

Regardless of your religious preference or spiritual bias, you cannot deny the monumental impact Jesus has made upon civilization throughout history. Ironically, His leading only lasted approximately three years. He never led an army or organized anything resembling a corporate flowchart. Jesus never wrote a book or traveled more than a few miles from His birthplace. Yet more has been spoken and written about this Man than anyone else in history.

If you study the methodology of His work, you either describe it as supremely lucky, sheer genius, or divinely blessed. Most of Jesus's activity took place in a small group of 12. The secret behind groups of 4 to 12 meeting consistently for personal growth and support has been discovered by many throughout the ages. Perhaps the most significant benefit is personal responsibility. Putting ourselves in charge of our own soul growth is akin to putting the fox in charge of the chicken coop. The world has little room or patience for people who are self-righteous and oblivious to their own needs. Joining a small group will constantly remind you of your need for God and others. We cannot do it alone.

The main reason people avoid small groups for spiritual growth, prayer, Bible study, and mutual accountability is that they don't want to be responsible for spiritual development. They don't want people to know them, to see any weaknesses, or to nudge them out of their spiritual comfort zones. Most people are blinded to their needs for growth because they avoid situations where they will be forced to see and deal with their inadequacies. We can bluff others in public settings, but we cannot do so for very long in effective small groups.

The challenge of leaders is to find small-group members who will not only challenge them spiritually, but who are also safe to be around. Meeting with either superiors or subordinates can be politically dangerous and can thwart group process. Meeting with peers can create a competitive atmosphere unless the peers are from outside the organization or field. The bottom line is that leaders need to either seek out or create small-group involvement where they are most likely to benefit spiritually. Faith-based groups are places to dialogue about Sunday sermons, books, or truth applications. There is nothing like a well-led small group for the purpose of enhancing spiritual growth. While it is no substitute for personal time with God and corporate worship, the small group is the best proven vehicle for enhancing spiritual growth. Exceptional leaders get involved in small groups for the purpose of developing themselves as people. Developed people develop people best.

Shell 3: Use the Bible as a Spiritual Guide

Sailors have their north star, timekeepers their Greenwich Mean Time, and carpenters their tape measures. Every

WHILE EXCELLENT LEADERS NEED NOT BE THEOLOGIANS, BECOMING FAMILIAR WITH THE BIBLE IS CRUCIAL TO MAXIMUM LEADERSHIP.

trade has its go-to instrument that provides direction, consistency, and guidance. Morality has to do with how we deal with people and our creator. Because leaders are inherently in the people business, they need a guide for understanding values, morality, and spirituality. While many time-tested principles exist, those contained in the Bible provide a perfect place to start. The Bible offers all the basic necessities for fleshing out the details, which is a responsibility of leaders.

Leaders become the conscience for the organizations they lead. If they lack a systematic approach to right and wrong, people tend to gravitate to the lowest common denominator. If stealing is okay in certain situations, then people will steal. If lying seems justified in a given context, then deceit becomes the norm. When love is not valued, people will gossip, bicker, fight, and mistrust one another. When this happens, teamwork will usually become nonexistent. The Founding Fathers of America understood the need for moral and spiritual guidelines that superseded their own wisdom. A commonly adopted guide to provide direction for how we treat people and property was needed.

That is why we see so many inscriptions from the Bible on our old government buildings. Our early leaders knew what many of us have yet to learn: There cannot be a value-free society. You cannot live civilly and have laws that elevate the value of life without some sort of moral guide.

Divorce God-given values from any society, and you wreck families, bankrupt organizations, and lead a culture into chaos. Any strong society must acknowledge some formal moral guide on which to establish its values, which, in turn, results in good everyday decisions.

While excellent leaders need not be theologians, becoming familiar with the Bible is crucial to maximum leadership. If you want to lead with your whole being, you must include your soul. You cannot lead spiritually without a system for spiritual growth.

Take Bible study seriously. Make your own notes in the margins of your Bible as you read and listen to sermons. Listen to well-respected speakers and read books with classic Christian themes. Effective leaders recognize the need to use the Bible as a spiritual guide for the purpose of becoming well rounded.

Here are some superb books to choose from as you develop this important aspect of your leadership potential:

- *Mere Christianity* by C.S. Lewis

- *More Than a Carpenter* by Josh McDowell

- *What the Bible Is All About* by Henrietta Mears

- *The Case for Christianity* by Lee Strobel

- *Victory over the Darkness* by Neil T. Anderson

- *The Pursuit of God* by A.W. Tozer

- *How to Be a Christian Without Being Religious* by Fritz Ridenour

- *Orthodoxy* by G.K. Chesterton

- *Prayer* by O. Hallesby

- *The Practice of the Presence of God* by Brother Lawrence

- *No Wonder They Call Him the Savior* by Max Lucado

- *Confessions* by St. Augustine

- *The Cost of Discipleship* by Dietrich Bonhoeffer

- *Disappointment with God* by Philip Yancey

- *My Utmost for His Highest* by Oswald Chambers

- *Fasting for Spiritual Breakthrough* by Elmer Towns

- *The Cycle of Victorious Living* by Earl and Hazel Lee

Shell 4: Participate in a Vibrant Faith Community

Participating in a vibrant faith community is different from "going to church." Religious institutions abound, but many do not have the sort of spiritual energy and authentic focus on God that justifies significant involvement. Sitting through a religious service just to get your ticket punched is not a good use of your time. Do your homework. Seek out a place where you can sense the spiritual energy, where the Bible is clearly communicated in ways you can relate to it. Look for people who exude an attitude that would make you want to invite your friends, family, and work associates to spend time with them.

Forget about finding the perfect congregation, pastor, or staff. They don't exist. As someone once said, "If you found the perfect church, you'd ruin it by attending." Rather, pick a place that provides consistent, challenging soul growth. Get involved in a place of service; do not just spectate. Effective leaders do not try to lead all the time. They also submit, learn, serve, and choose to be good followers. This is the sort of soul-development activity you need if you are to lead spiritually. Just as leaders need people and develop organizations, so faith grows best in the context of relationships and group worship.

Lone Ranger God-followers rarely amount to much spiritually. They do not have the stamina to make it through the temptations and tough times. It's similar to why you can find so much slightly used home exercise equipment at garage sales. The very oldest social organization is the local parish, where people of faith gather together because of the one thing they all hold dear: their need for a God connection. Do not underestimate the importance of spiritual discipline. Make it your mission. Work your soul, just as you exercise your body, mind, and talents. Lazy employees make poor team members; lazy parishioners make lousy faith communities. Spiritual fruit does not just happen—it has to be cultivated.

At the same time you nurture your soul through active involvement in a faith community, affirm that kind of behavior in those you lead. The best team members are growing, whole, spiritually dynamic people. When God works in the lives of other team members, it creates a positive energy throughout the entire team. Attitude improves and complaining decreases. Honesty is enhanced and deceptiveness is reduced. Instead of gossip and slander, love and forgiveness become characteristic of internal relations, which any leader knows is a plus in terms of esprit de corps. People without inner peace find difficulty in maintaining peace in their relationships. Morality, self-esteem, and relationship issues improve.

Shell 5: Minister to the Souls of Team Members

The twenty-first century is being led by people who appreciate the spiritual dimension of their lives and with growing concern want to live and work around organizations that do not deny this aspect of their being. Therefore, if you are to be effective in leading in our current age, you must think of yourself as a minister more than ever before. It's Christ's leadership in a life rather than a clergy certificate that makes someone able to minister to others. With so much family dysfunction, personal problems, and moral damage in society, leaders cannot pretend that people check these things at the door when they get involved in organizational matters. Leaders must care for the souls as well as the emotional and relational needs of the people they lead.

This care must be genuine. Otherwise, it amounts to little more than organizational prostitution: valuing people based simply on their talents, skills, or abilities, disregarding what gives them true value as humans. Every person is made in the image of God. Every team member is a person with dreams, feelings, and fears. Pretending these do not exist or ignoring them as outside the bounds of your leadership will limit your entire team's potential. Thus, for the sake of the organization, exceptional leaders elevate concern for the whole person. While most organizations are not dedicated solely to spiritual development, leaders must work hard not to diminish the value of a living person as a spiritual being.

Leaders, specifically, must see themselves as God's agents, designed to dispense grace where it's needed. Standing up for the underdogs, choosing the moral high road, and taking time to care for the needs of people are examples of establishing an atmosphere where spirituality is deemed valuable. Pray for those you lead. Lift them up to God. At appropriate times, let your teammates know you are praying for them. When people feel as though you care for them as individuals rather than just organizational cogs, they will grow in their respect, dedication, and enthusiasm. While these are not the primary reasons superior leaders care for people, they are desirable by-products.

Spiritual leaders need not be preachy Bible-thumpers. The last thing most people want is to be force-fed religion. But do not overreact to these negative stereotypes so much that you leave a spiritual void within your leading. The creator of the universe has endowed you with abilities and opportunities to represent Him among those you lead. Your responsibility is significant. Don't take it lightly.

You are ordained to influence others, and part of that power is spiritual in nature. Go, Reverend Leader.

7

THE LEADER'S MESSAGE

Learning Where to Look for Answers

Even though Paul had finished explaining the five areas of effective leading, Tim was excited to see his friend again. His son's sports schedule had required his family to miss a weekend at the beach. Tim arose early on the next Saturday morning, poured his mug of coffee, and went for a walk beside the ocean. As he neared Paul's house, he looked up to see an empty chair where his friend had perched each morning. He could not remember a time on his walks when Paul was not on his deck enjoying the morning sights and sounds of the beach.

Tim walked up to the landing at the bottom of the stairs near the deck and called out. "Paul, are you there?"

He climbed the stairs to the deck. The blinds were closed. He knocked on the door and called out again. "Paul? It's Tim." Glancing to his right he noticed the large starfish that Paul had hung on the wall for their talk times. Tim knocked a little louder.

"Hello!" a female voice called.

Tim turned around. A woman stood on the white sand by the house next to Paul's cottage.

"Good morning," Tim said. "I'm looking for Paul."

The woman said, "Oh, I'm so sorry. You must not have heard."

"Heard what?"

"Paul passed away last week."

Tim fought back the tears as he moved from the deck toward the woman. "What…what happened?"

"He had been battling a brain tumor for the last year or so. He was growing weak the last couple of months, but I guess complications set in and he went quickly."

"Wow. I was just with him a couple weeks ago. We've spent the last five Saturdays talking. He seemed so vibrant."

"He was a sweet and intelligent man. You must be the young friend Paul told me about before he was taken to the hospital. I would come over and check on him a couple times a day. Before he took a turn for the worst, he gave me an envelope and asked me to give it to a new friend he had met named Tim."

"That's my name."

"Let me get it for you." She disappeared inside her house next door and returned with a manila envelope. "Tim" had been printed on the front with a large black marker. The woman handed it to Tim, who was now standing on the edge of her beach deck.

"Thank you," he said. "I still can't believe it. I didn't know Paul was that sick. I assumed he might be ailing from something, but he never mentioned his illness."

"He wouldn't. I'm so sorry you didn't know, Tim, but Paul was a scrapper, and he hardly ever complained. Even when he did, he did it in a jovial manner. He was one of those rare, special souls you get the pleasure of meeting in life. I'm sorry I have to be the one to tell you the news. His family came this week to take away his things. Your envelope is all I have."

"Thanks so very much. I'm sure Paul appreciated all the help you gave him."

"It was my privilege."

Tim walked away from the house, looking up one more time at the starfish on the wall as he clutched the envelope with his name on it. He strolled slowly toward his house.

Even though he had only met Paul a short time ago, he felt as if he had known him for years. The depth of Paul's wisdom and the intensity of his beliefs made Tim feel that way. He couldn't believe Paul was gone. He was sad he would not have an opportunity to see him and tell him how much he appreciated the mentoring.

Tim approached his rented beach house and sat down on the sand. Leaning against the retaining wall with his coffee mug in his left hand, he stared at the waves as they crashed one after the other onto the shore. Seagulls flew overhead, and birds chirped in the trees. Time seemed to stand still.

Carefully he looked at the envelope. The contents felt like a book, thick and heavy. He slowly slid his finger under the tab at one end and opened it. He reached inside and grabbed the contents. He pulled out a thin black leather book that looked like a Bible. He held up the envelope and peered inside. That was all. He looked at the spine of the book, *Holy Bible*. Why had Paul given him a Bible?

Tim noticed a card sticking out of the top of the book. He put his finger on the card and flipped open the Bible. Instantly smiling, he observed that the card was a photo of a starfish lying on the seashore. He turned it over. In shaky letters, Paul had written a message: *I believe in you, Tim.*

You're already on the way to becoming a highly effective leader. See you in eternity. —Paul. Tears welled up in Tim's eyes as he held the book and looked at the postcard.

Looking down at the open Bible, Tim noted where the card had been placed. The title read 1 Timothy. Chapter 1 began, "Paul, an apostle of Christ Jesus by the command of God our Savior and of Christ Jesus our hope, to Timothy my true son in the faith: Grace, mercy and peace from God the Father and Christ Jesus our Lord" (verses 1-2).

Tim began to turn the pages. He stopped. Two pages later was a passage that had been highlighted. He read the passage aloud.

> Don't let anyone look down on you because you are young, but set an example for the believers in speech, in conduct, in love, in faith and in purity. Until I come, devote yourself to the public reading of Scripture, to preaching and to teaching. Do not neglect your gift, which was given you through prophecy when the body of elders laid their hands on you. Be diligent in these matters; give yourself wholly to them, so that everyone may see your progress. Watch your life and doctrine closely. Persevere in them, because if you do, you will save both yourself and your hearers (1 Timothy 4:12-16).

Tim closed the Bible and looked at the horizon. "Paul?" he whispered with a smile. "I'll see you again in eternity, my friend. But until then, I'll do my best to be a godly leader and a person of excellence."

> *In everything he did he had great success,*
> *because the Lord was with him.*
>
> 1 Samuel 18:14

FINAL WORD

The writer of this book has had the privilege of observing these principles of leadership at every level, from Main Street business owners to national political and sports leaders. His ultimate model for leading is Jesus, who "did not come to be served, but to serve, and to give his life as a ransom for many" (Mark 10:45). In order to be the kind of leader described in this book, develop a personal relationship with God through His Son, the historical, biblical Jesus. It's as simple as ABC.

Acknowledge your need to make things right with God. "For all have sinned and fall short of the glory of God" (Romans 3:23). Sin is defined as moral or spiritual failure of any kind, separating us all from a holy God.

Believe that Jesus Christ died to pay the price for you. "Yet to all who did receive him, to those who believed in his name, he gave the right to become children of God" (John 1:12). His death did what no number of good deeds could ever do—pay the price necessary to provide us with forgiveness from God and access to Him.

Confess your faith in Jesus Christ as the one leader of your life. "If you declare with your mouth, 'Jesus is Lord,' and believe in your heart that God raised him from the dead, you will be saved" (Romans 10:9).

> *Dear God, I need You. I know I am not right with You. Please forgive my moral and spiritual failures. I believe that Your Son, Jesus, came to die for me, paying the price of my sin with His own life—all because of Your great love for me. I now turn from my self-led life and invite You to be my leader. Amen.*

NOTEBOOK

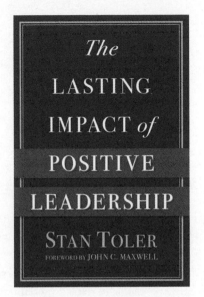

The
LASTING
IMPACT *of*
POSITIVE
LEADERSHIP

STAN TOLER

FOREWORD BY JOHN C. MAXWELL

GREAT TEAMS START WITH GREAT LEADERS

You know that nobody succeeds alone—you need a great team. But when you're the leader and you aren't sure how to nurture the best from your crew, where can you turn for help?

In *The Lasting Impact of Positive Leadership*, bestselling author Stan Toler serves as your coach and reveals what it takes to build a successful team. As you examine the proven strategies of great leaders, you will learn how to effectively connect and communicate, and how to motivate people and inspire them to give their best every day.

Creating a positive culture starts with learning how to harness the principles of positive leadership. Become a positive leader...and discover for yourself the remarkable results that are sure to follow!

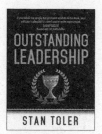

TOOLS TO HELP YOU BECOME
A TRANSFORMATIONAL LEADER

What makes a leader stand out? What are the keys to truly making a difference? And how can you become the influencer you were created to be?

With more than 40 years of leadership experience, Stan Toler knows what it takes to empower people to reach organizational and personal goals. He cuts through the mystery and confusion and provides clear guidelines to help you accomplish vital leadership tasks, including...

- defining your vision, developing your plan, and communicating clearly to help people buy in to your shared goal

- overcoming common leadership challenges to create a culture of success

- building strong relationships and effective teams that make working hard worthwhile

You'll find all the tools, tips, and practical guidance you need to help individuals and groups reach their highest potential and fulfill their God-given purpose.

MAKE THE MOST OF YOUR
OPPORTUNITIES TO BUILD OTHERS UP

You don't need to be big or bold to impact those around you. By recognizing your ability to be a positive influence, you unlock your power to change lives for the better.

With more than 3 million copies of his books in print, bestselling author Stan Toler is a trusted voice on leadership and making a difference. In *The Power of Your Personal Impact*, Stan examines how you can profoundly change the world you live in. This book will help you...

- develop a vision and purpose for your future

- discover ways to motivate others using kindness and compassion

- encourage people to achieve greatness in their own lives

Your words, actions, and attitudes hold the strength to leave a lasting impression. *The Power of Your Personal Impact* will help you understand how to make the most of your gifts as you use them to inspire others.

KEEPING A CLEAR VISION AND A SHARP FOCUS

You are a leader—people look to you to be an example, offer direction, and provide inspiration. But with so much to do, how can you keep fresh, focused, and excited about your opportunity to make a difference in people's lives?

Bestselling author Stan Toler provides inspirational quotes, one-page gems of wisdom, and memorable taglines to fuel your passion and clarify your vision. You'll find plenty of helpful reminders that...

- Leaders are in the people business. As a leader, your primary function is not to buy, sell, or ply a trade. It is to understand and work with people.

- Bureaucrats run institutions. Leaders lead people. You can make the difference.

- Leadership is a team sport. Do more than direct individuals—build a team.

This treasure of tried-and-true principles will be your on-the-go source for the motivation and encouragement you need be the effective leader you were created to be.

A MENTOR TO HELP YOU REACH THE NEXT LEVEL

It's tough to find a strong mentor who can provide the counsel and encouragement you need to feel confident in yourself and your choices. But it doesn't have to be that way! From bestselling author Stan Toler, *Minute Motivators for Men* is a playbook for living up to the standard of excellence.

Receive daily guidance on how you can be your best, including how you can...

- take charge by taking control of your attitude

- lead with gentle strength wherever you go

- express your feelings—from anger to gratitude—in honest and constructive ways

If you desire to grow in your character and capability, you'll find many powerful and effective tips here. *Minute Motivators for Men* will inspire you to become the leader, husband, father, and friend you've always wanted to be.

STAN TOLER &
LINDA TOLER

Minute
Motivators
for
Women

*Quick Inspiration for the
Time of Your Life*

BE REFRESHED...ANY MINUTE OF YOUR DAY

Whether you pick up this book first thing in the morning or when you're winding down at bedtime, you'll be inspired and encouraged over and over again!

Bestselling author Stan Toler and his wife, Linda, share thought-provoking quotes and beautiful words of hope within these pages. Each chapter will draw your attention to a single attribute every godly woman wants to cultivate in her life, such as patience, wisdom, persistence, courage, and gratitude.

Bite-size portions of inspiration make this the perfect devotional for, well, anytime—especially those days when you feel like you can never get ahead. Recharge in the middle of a hectic schedule or end your day with a much-needed reminder that God has every aspect of your life under control.

ABOUT THE AUTHOR

Stan Toler has spoken in over 90 countries and written over 100 books with sales of more than 3 million copies. Toler for many years served as vice president and instructor for John C. Maxwell's INJOY Leadership Institute, training leaders how to make a difference in the world.

To learn more about Harvest House books and
to read sample chapters, visit our website:

www.HarvestHousePublishers.com

HARVEST HOUSE PUBLISHERS
EUGENE, OREGON